# EMOTIONAL INTELLIGENCE MADE SIMPLE

8 books in 1:

How to Analyze and Influence People,
Cognitive Behavioral Therapy, NLP,
Mental Models, Critical Thinking,
Empath, Self-Esteem, Psychology 101

BY

*Gary Scott*

# TABLE OF CONTENTS

# CHAPTER 1

# HOW TO ANALYZE AND INFLUENCE PEOPLE

# Secrets of Psychologists to Read People As If They Were Open Books

Surely you have wished more than once to be able to read other people's minds. Some are saved with the help of their developed intuition, but if you are not so conscious, you only have one way out: learn to decipher body language.

It is no longer a secret that with the help of nonverbal communication, we get 55 percent of the information. Allan Pease, the famous Australian writer, mentioned it more than once. Expressions of the face, gestures, and body movements can remove the mask from anyone, revealing their real thoughts and feelings.

The wording of Genial. Guru proposes you to pay attention to the signals sent to us by the people around us without even knowing it.

## 1. Closing the eyes

If a person, speaking with you, closes his eyes, you have to know that he is trying to hide or protect himself from the outside world. This does not mean that I fear you. Rather, the other way around. He wants to take you out of his field of vision. You may have bored it already. Close your eyes and bam! You disappeared.

## 2. Protecting the mouth by hand

It is a vivid example that we all come from childhood. Remember, how you covered your mouth with the palm of your hand when you didn't want to say something. An adult is the same. Some fingers, palm, or fist help us contain the words. Sometimes we mask it with a simulated cough.

## 3. Biting the ring of your glasses

Is a friend of yours thoughtfully biting the rings of his glasses? Try to support and encourage him. Surely you will be worried about something and at your subconscious level try to feel safe, as in childhood with the mother's breast. By the way, a pencil, pen, finger, cigarette, or even chewing gum in the mouth also indicates the same.

## 4. Showing face

Many women use this gesture to attract the attention of men. Supporting the chin on the folded hands, we expose our face to show it, as if it were the shop window in a store as if we were saying: "Here I am so pretty, admire me." Men should remember this gesture so as not to miss the opportunity to make a compliment on time.

## 5. Stroking the chin

In this way, the person tries to make a decision. At the same time, your gaze can be directed down, up, to the left, or any other side. He does not realize what he sees at that precise moment since he is completely immersed in his thoughts.

## 6. Crossed arms

It is one of the most common gestures. It is not surprising that many people feel very comfortable with this pose since this gesture helps to isolate themselves from others. Many times we use it when we are not comfortable with something. The crossed arms are a clear sign of the negative attitude of your interlocutor.

## 7. Exposing oneself

This pose is more open. When a woman wants to like a man, she starts exposing herself by showing her the best sides. She straightens to highlight her breasts and crosses her legs. The folded arms below are a clear signal of attention towards the interlocutor.

## 8. Leaning forward

When a person feels sympathy for his interlocutor and wants to have contact with him or her, he usually leans forward. At the same time, the feet may remain in the same place, but the body advances instinctively.

## 9. Leaning back

If the person leans against the back of his seat, he makes it clear that he is bored with the conversation. You may feel uncomfortable in the presence of your interlocutor.

## 10. Toe, heel

Yes, adults do too. Not only children. This gesture indicates that the person is anxious.

## 11. Rubbing his hands

It is said that the hands convey what the head thinks. When we rub our hands, we usually express expectations or hope of some success in something. In other words, we make this gesture when we think about future benefits.

## 12. Handshake "glove"

If your interlocutor greeting you grabs you with both hands, it shows that you can trust him.

## 13. Squeeze with palm up

The palm-up, covering the interlocutor's hand, indicates empathy, but only if done at once. If the hands were already held for a specific moment and then someone put the palm up, it may indicate their desire to show who is in charge.

## 14. Squeeze with palm down

By supporting your caller's hand, it is as if you were talking about your willingness to help him.

## 15. Squeeze with a touch

With the available hand, the person can touch the forearm,

elbow, or the back of the person he is greeting. This invasion of personal space shows the need for communication. And the closer the body is, the higher the need.

### 16. Straightening the tie

Here everything depends on the situation. If it is a man who does it in the presence of a woman, it is highly possible that he likes it. But this gesture can also mean that the person does not feel comfortable. You might have lied or want to leave.

### 17. Collecting non-existent hairs

It is thus called the gesture of repression. Most of the time, people use it to express their tacit disagreement. In other words, they do not openly express their opinion, but they certainly do not agree with what is happening around them.

### 18. Feet on the table

This gesture can mean many things: bad manners, disrespect, desire to show off as a great boss, or concern for your health. However, psychologists tend to believe that even if you feel very comfortable in this position. it would be better if you use it at home or in the presence of your family.

### 19. Riding the chair

A chair is not a horse and its back, although in some ways it seems, is not a shield. Also, it was made for other purposes.

So many people are bothered by this way of sitting around because, at the intuitive level, we feel a lot of aggression from the "mounted" person. Typically, dominant people use this position.

## 20. Playing with the shoe

Cross-legged is one of the most attractive female poses. And if we add to him playing with the shoe half removed, we accentuate it even more. This gesture speaks of a relaxed and calm mood and serves as a kind of green traffic light for man.

## 21. Eye contact

The eyes are the mirror of the soul and a perfect instrument of communication. There we can read all the feelings and emotions of the interlocutor. Lovers stare into each other's eyes, unconsciously waiting to see how they get bigger. And this shows a lot because the pupils can increase in size up to 4 times, compared to their normal state. And, by the way, if the person gets angry, their eyes become like accounts due to the maximum reduction of the pupils.

# How to Analyze A Person By Their Photos

Have you just met someone, added you to their Facebook, Twitter, or Instagram, and are you wondering what kind of personality you have? Do you want to know what message you give the world with your photographs on the networks?

Since the arrival of the Internet in our lives, the way we have to relate to others has changed radically. Now we have space where others can see what we want them to see. The images we decided to upload to our social networks show much more than we imagine. An Internet profile is a projection of what we want to show the world, our desires, and even our insecurities. That is why, by making a correct analysis of the published photos, we can develop an accurate personality profile.

Tell me what profile picture you have, and I will tell you how you are.

**What the profile photos indicate**

When we choose a profile picture (whether for WhatsApp, Facebook, Instagram...), we are choosing our cover letter to the world. After that election, there is a series of mental processes that arise to avoid giving an image that we don't want to give. For example, someone more introvert will have more difficulties in this process, and they may not change their photographs very often. In extreme cases, these people hide behind anonymous profiles.

Some elements that we can analyze from the profile photos are the following:

- **Pose:** people who are not afraid to expose themselves usually go out with open arms, calm and with full-length (or half-body) photographs. However, a more reserved person probably has a more serious photograph, with arms crossed and in a more closed plane.
- **Facial expression:** a wide smile, without touch-ups and head-on, they are usually self-confident, open, and outgoing people. A grimace may be a sign that we want to show "naturalness" but, deep down, we feel insecure and force ourselves to be funny in a photograph. The most serious people (or who use their networks for professional purposes) usually leave with a half-smile or, wIth an expression without grimaces and sober.
- **If we go out with more people:** going out with many people in the photo can indicate a tendency to be sociable, they enjoy life more in the company, and a photo alone does not represent them.
- **If it is a photo with our partner:** although the image we give on the networks about our partner is not reality, uploading many photos or having a profile picture with your partner does not imply anything bad, on the contrary. A photo with our partner means that we have taken the step of showing the world

who we are united with and who is part of our life.

- **If it is an old or childhood photo:** these types of images indicate a strong anchor to the past, we may be going through a bad time and do not want to connect with it or, we are simply afraid to move on in our lives.
- **Photo color:** color is also a crucial element; a black and white photo can be a sign of a melancholic, poetic, or introverted personality. On the other hand, bright colors usually express vitality and joy.
- **If the photo is not of us:** some people hide behind anonymous profiles, avatars of soccer players, celebrities, or cartoons. These individuals travel through the networks without interest to show their personality, either because of fear, insecurities, or because they do not like to show their lives to a vast audience.

## The psychology of colors in profile photos

The study of how colors affect our lives has also reached the analysis of personality, the ones we choose for our virtual presentation letter also show very characteristic features of us.

## Black and white photos

As we have commented previously, a black and white photo can be a sign of melancholy and artistic tendencies. Retouching a photograph to remove the shades can also indicate bad self-esteem and, as a consequence, certain insecurity when showing us the world.

## Photos with lots of colors

The strident photos, with many shades and full of color, are characteristics of equally strident and striking people. Not only is it a sign of extraversion, but the striking colors also indicate the desire to attract attention and to have a certain presence in the lives of others, whether in the real world or on the Internet.

## Photos with blue tones

Using cold tones such as blue can indicate two things: either a corporate personality, sober and elegant, or a tendency to be a cold and calculating person. These tones do not invite you to delve into the personal depths of each one.

## Photos with red color

If this striking tone predominates in the photo, we may want to show the energy and passion we have in our day to day. The use of warm colors denotes an intense, competitive, and sometimes aggressive personality.

## Half-face photos: meaning

Not showing our face partially can indicate two very different things:

- **Mysterious personality:** half-face invites you to enter the profile to discover more, see what that person hides and reveal his personality.

- **Disinterest in social networks:** a person who does not mind being exposed to social networks but does not want to waste time on them. For this type of individual, a half-face photo implies that they have given the message that they don't want to show their whole life on it.

**Back photo: meaning**

It is possible that in the profile picture, we do not even want to face, the back photos reflect a certain level of resistance when having social networks and being active in them. In this type of photos, the face is not visible and, therefore, we hide our facial expressions from the world of the Internet.

On the other hand, a photo from behind can also mean that we have gone through a painful time. Right now, we do not have enough courage to show ourselves in the face of a world as extensive as social networks.

Finally, it is worth mentioning that, although it is interesting to know how to analyze a person by their photos. Each individual is a world, a very intricate set of experiences and paths, and that it is better to talk to a person if we want to know them thoroughly.

# Five Major Factors Analyzing Personality, According

# To Goldberg

Lewis Goldberg's personality theory is also known as the "Big Five Model." It stems from a variety of studies in which the excellence of a particular personality trait is repeated as a factor determining people's way of life. I have been talking about this model since 1933, but it was 1993 that was structured as a theory.

The five main personality traits are identified by capital letters and are also known as "main factors." The first is the element of "O" —openness to new experiences. The second is the responsibility of "C." The third is "E" or extrovert. The room is "A" or kind. And finally, the fifth is "N" or emotional instability. The letters from the acronym "OCEAN."

Each one is like a god, but you can leave it to God. "

-Miguel Servet-

Similarly, each of these characteristics is made up of more specific features. From this model, a variety of personality tests have been developed that can evaluate and measure how people have evaluated. Let's take a closer look at the features and characteristics of the model.

**Openness to experience, one of the personality traits**

Openness to experience ("O") refers to the ability to find new skills, space them in life and creatively visualize the future. Those who have this level at a high level are imaginative people who appreciate art and collaborate with others. They are also curious and prefer variations over every day.

The opposite is people who have closed to an experience they have never experienced before. The opposition characterizes them. This means that they prefer a guaranteed traditional one. They prefer strict routines because they take time to adapt to new things. They tend to be technical and tend to show little interest in abstraction.

**Responsibility or factor "C"**

This dimension relates to self-control ability and the ability to develop effective ways of acting. It refers to the ability to plan, organize, and execute tasks. You must also be able to achieve your goals, keep on time, and maintain your goals and goals.

People with high scores in this dimension are often seen as organized, reliable, and demanding people. Taking this personality trait to extremes can lead to perfectionism and even work addiction. They feel a great need to succeed.

**Extraversion, another personality trait**

It has to do with having fun with other people's companies. People who have this most prominent feature feel comfortable when they are with others and act in harmony when they are in a group. They are good people working in teams, optimistic and enthusiastic. Along with others, they are like sea fish.

There is an introverted person on the other side, and it is best to work alone. Often, you feel certain distrust and attention to others. They prefer a small circle of friends and are very uncomfortable with a large group.

**"A" factor: kindness**

Mainly related to empathy. Those who show excellence in this personality factor understand, forgive, and calm with others. Demonstrate your ability to understand other people's needs and feelings.

The people on the other side are in conflict. These are people who like discussion and debate and want to give their perspective. Hostility is your brand. They can work well in activities that require demonstrations of competition and energetic attitudes towards others.

**Emotional instability or neurosis**

It specifically talks about the ability or lack of ability that one has to overcome in the face of difficult life situations. People who show a high level of this factor are characterized by unpredictable behavior. They do not maintain a series of actions, but the reasons are not very clear, and their reactions are different.

On the opposite end, some stable people remain attentive and modest in critical situations. They are quiet people who are relieved with the ability to handle difficulties and mistakes. Your emotional state is positive, even in the face of problems.

# Read People and See-Through

Honestly, wouldn't it be nice to be able to assess people with lightning speed and to know immediately how to deal with the best? Which buttons do you have to press to reach what you want?

You know instantly which kind of person you are dealing with and which behavior is likely to happen to you from a few perceptions. This knowledge gives you a huge informational edge, while the other person is still completely in the dark, not knowing the number of inferences on their personality you have already learned.

Your ability to perceive what others have missed reading between the lines, after a few sentences, will allow you to get a clear picture of a person and place them in a grid that will allow you to predict the person's remaining attributes and preferences. In short, you can read people and see what really drives them.

Would not that be an incredibly helpful skill? Just think about what this knowledge could bring you benefits. In which situations would you have the decisive advantage? In which situations could you have prevented so much, if you had already known in advance, how a person would probably act? And with which people would it be much easier if you knew exactly how you should deal with them?

We, humans, love to look for patterns in our environment and to recognize them.

Scientifically this tendency is called "Randomness Error". It is one of the automatically occurring attention mistakes that cause us to perceive the reality a bit distorted. In a nutshell, he says that we assign meaning to random events that they do not have. They just happened completely arbitrarily.

However, we try to make sense of everything and therefore recognize seemingly recurrent patterns that help us to categorize events in our environment. Even though these categories often do not exist. And of course, we do the same with our fellow human beings and their behaviors. Of course, this has some advantages and disadvantages.

Classifying people makes their behavior more manageable and allows us to rate the unknown. This seems to be an inherent pattern of human behavior. Evolutionary conditionally was necessary to detect dangers early. Today, it helps us to be better at dealing with people and to assess how they will behave. It allows us to be one step ahead of others.

Already in ancient Greece, the personality of the people was classified in the grid of the temperament theory. Similar to the personality types, according to Carl Gustav Jung, the Myers-Briggs type indicator, or the "Big 5" of the OCEAN model, which is often used in psychology today, people of every segment were given certain qualities.

By recognizing some of these typical behaviors or characteristics, people can be assigned to a segment. Once assigned, one knows which other behaviors and characteristics the classified person is now statistically most likely to have and how best to deal with it.

Of course, this knowledge has not only advantages but also significant disadvantages. Katja Vogt once said that in all the drawers that we humans entertain, unfortunately, only a sock is lost.

This quote nicely reminds us that too hasty conclusions can often have consequences, and many things pass us because of our now active expectation filter. We should, therefore, pay very close attention to whether the model used allows me to assign other unerring drawers.

In our opinion, the models mentioned above have some upgradable points that need to be considered when trying to "categorize" people. First, categorizing bothers us.

We in the NLP are convinced that we can always only recognize tendencies. The world is not black and white; it shows in many shades. And so do personality traits of people.

The second point is that we humans can change and evolve. Such an analysis is static. Just as an exam is just a snapshot, a survey or questionnaire can capture our personality at some point in time based on a set of criteria.

But because NLP itself is a dynamic model and we constantly calibrate our conversational waking ears and sharp eye in conversations and situations, we can easily perceive changes and deviant behavior.

NLP's behavioral analysis is always up-to-date, and its users are aware that human behavior is constantly changing, but they have the ability to respond flexibly to these changes.

Also, many analysis models overlook the fact that human behavior is very context-dependent. I can take the helm in a situation and lead a group safely to the desired point.

Likewise, in a different context, I can sit back, wait and see what the others do, and talk and engage only when I have a clear picture of the situation. Just because I got things going in a context and was virtually the "doer" does not mean that I do that in any other context, let alone that it always makes sense.

**But how can I analyze and read people and their behavior with NLP?**

The model we use is called MBC - Meta Behavioral Coding. It is our creation and combines the best elements of some well tested and working analysis models.

These include, for example, the metaprogramming from the NLP, which is derived from it specifically for the working context of Dr. med. Rodger Bailey derived LAB® Profiles (Language and Behavior Profiles) and some analysis tools used in profiling and the military.

With MBC, we use a framework that allows us to

incorporate human behavior into over 20 facets. Based on the different characteristics and metaprogram combinations, we can assess ourselves and our counterpart very precisely and derive action strategies.

You already know one of the metaprograms if the VAKOG model tells you something. This metaprogram tells you from the language of a human in which sensory channels your counterpart perceives his environment and thus also in which sensory channels you should talk to this person in order to create a good basis for conversation and to prevent one another from talking to one another. Here you can find more about the VAKOG model.

Metaprograms themselves are, therefore, unconscious personality patterns and filters of our brain. These determine our behavior, how we are motivated, how we make decisions, how we value things, and how we perceive our environment. Metaprograms thus help us to see how our counterpart is sorting his reality and what his subconscious personality patterns look like.

Of course, these patterns have a powerful impact on how and what we talk about. From the structure of a person's language, MBC allows us to create precisely those unconscious patterns to hear and to get insights into the personality. A small example. Markus and Christina have just a small disagreement at a meeting.

**Markus says:** "Before we start, we have to rethink our decisions and analyze together whether we have thought everything through. We can not risk external factors bugging us. "

**Christina says:** "Thinking, even more, does not make sense. We finally have to get started; we're running out of time. We will already be able to handle the external factors when the time comes."

Here different metaprogramming meets, which causes conflicts more frequently. We're talking about the meta-program Proactive/Reactive. We want to introduce you to this today.

Proactive people are action-oriented and take initiative. They want to do something. The activity and the action are in the foreground. Precise analysis of the situation and the most accurate balancing of all available alternatives usually leave it to others. Much can only be considered for them once you have started. They assume that they have a handle on what happens and can influence environmental factors through their behavior.

In everyday life, they are often referred to as "makers," as they initiate many ideas and take the first steps. This is helpful when an action is required. In extreme cases, the quick start and initiate actions can also happen rashly and anger other people. It may seem that they act like "steamrolling" and could have prevented some with a little more thought in advance.

Leave reactive people to take the initiative to other people. Situations have to "mature" for them to make decisions.

They like to let things take theirs to see what impact this has on them. Situations want to be understood and analyzed before an action is taken. Reactive people also need to be completely sure that they have considered all alternatives. They see themselves in the area of the tension of external influences and find that environmental factors influence their behavior.

In everyday life, they are often referred to as "analysts" or "thinkers." They provide valuable solutions and a sharp analysis of problems. The honor of putting the first stone but May like to take another person. In extreme cases, this metaprogram can lead to an "analysis" loop, as there is always new input to analyze and understand.

There is no action at all until it is too late. Sometimes, other people also perceive reactive people as "passive" because they spend a lot of time waiting and contemplating. This can also make them passengers of their own lives.

So you realize that both Metaprograms have their advantages and disadvantages, none is better than the other. Depending on the situation or task, one expression can prove to be more advantageous than the other. Just ask yourself what expressions Mark and Christina have and how you can recognize them.

**How do I know which characteristic my counterpart has?**

Proactive:

Are very active in body language and movements, linguistically noticeable by short, sometimes incomplete sentences. Has problems staying calm for a long time.

- Typical sets of proactive people:
- What are we waiting for? Here we go!
- Now it's time to get started.
- Let's get started.

Reactive:

Tended to lean back more often or in a classic analysis posture. Speaks slowly and in longer, nested sentences. Longer inactive phrases are no problem.

Typical sentences of reactive persons:
- Let's look at precisely what we are dealing with here.
- We should think about that again before we do something.
- Let us also listen to other opinions on this topic.

**How can I use these patterns?**

Proactive people can be very well used as motivators and initiators of actions. They get things going and start where others are still thinking. But when there is a more prolonged standstill, they become impatient and try to get things moving. They can help get an otherwise reactive team going and prevent over-analysis.

Reactive people are excellent analysts; they weigh, want to understand and act thoughtfully. Especially in situations that need to be controlled in the background, or in an advisory capacity, it is recommended to use reactive persons. They can give proactive doer a clear direction and prevent essential things from being overlooked in a hurry. While the other one is starting to work, they can analyze further in the background and gradually work out new input.

**How can you best deal with proactive/reactive people?**

If you realize in a group process that proactive members are getting impatient and getting started, but the more reactive ones do not feel ready and need more time, then you can intervene very simply in this process. Split tasks and share the group is the magic formula.

Give the proactive something to do. Let them either fulfill smaller sub-goals or tasks that have already been agreed or give them tasks that need to be done either way. With them, you talk best about what has to be done and done. Once you've told them that, you do not have to worry about anything anymore; the tasks are done independently and quickly.

Thus, you give the reactive persons the time and opportunity to continue important analysis processes and give them the security they need. You give them to understand that this process wants to be carefully considered. With them too, it can help to use partial goals or milestones to make the analysis more precise and faster. Here it is important to set clear deadlines and execute them in order to prevent rethinking.

This way, the situation with Markus and Christina can easily be resolved. Both are focused on a common goal, and Christina can get started, while Markus can calmly devise strategies to tackle external factors. Of course, you explain their tasks to the two ineffective speech patterns that satisfy their metaprogramming.

Speech patterns that you can use to link to them include:

- **Christina:** Do, do, get started, act, now!
- **Markus:** Think, weigh, think, analyze, wait, act, when the time is right!

**What brings you now, MBC?**

In a nutshell: you can read carefully from the language of your conversation partners and recognize what they need and how they tick. So you know how to explain something "brain-friendly" in their language so that it makes sense to them intuitively and sounds good. You do not have to rely on a static personality analysis; you have the ability to calibrate your opponent's tendencies with a proven and simple grid at any time and in any context, and so have clear action strategies for you.

Imagine you are in a discussion and know what arguments will convince. In a negotiation, you realize how your demands are being accepted. What if you have to sell something and know exactly how to raise the need for it? Whether you want to motivate, lead, understand, or respond to someone, you will notice a noticeable difference and be able to prevent much in advance.

# How to Influence People

When we need to convince someone, we can use many techniques. Obviously, if we make a good proposal, we have valid arguments, and what we want to do is a win-win; it will be easy to convince our interlocutor of our interests.

But apart from the content, there are some small tricks that we can use to influence the people we talk to and achieve our goals.

The way we talk, our attitude, and know how to handle the conversation can be the key to getting a favorable response to our interest.

## 1. Smile

A smile on your face is the first thing we have to do if we want to influence people. When someone smiles, conveys happiness, and well, and we all like to feel good.

When a proposal is made with a smile on our face, we are more predisposed to accept what they are asking.

## 2. Take advantage of fatigue

When we are tired, we don't feel like arguing, and we are more willing to say yes (even if they leave us alone).

Cults know this perfectly. Therefore, the sessions where you "brainwash" are always long and exhausting. They know that a tired person has low defenses and is more willing to obey and accept how true what you are saying.

## 3. Make the ball

The ego is one of the weak points of all people. We all like to be told how good we are, and we are more willing to serve a person who makes us feel good.

It is not easy to flatter without it noticing. So, if you're beating someone to convince him, do it subtly and credibly.

## 4. Tell him many times YES

If you want to influence someone, let them say yes. When in a conversation, we say many times, yes, our brain understands that we are in tune with the person with whom we speak and the inertia of responding that if it can be an excellent tool to get us to respond affirmatively to what we want.

Cold-door commercials are one of the strategies they use very often:

- Do you want the best for your family? Yes
- Do you like to save on the fixed expenses of your home? Yes
- Do you live in this address? Yes
- Do you like things to work correctly? Yes
- Do you want me to make a special offer for you? Yes

Make the ball and let us say many times IF they are two of

the basic techniques of commercials.

## 5. Do not take the reason from your interlocutor

Showing someone who is not right in what he says and that if you have, it is an excellent strategy to feel good and have the feeling of "having won the argument."

But it is not an excellent strategy to influence another person.

When we argue, most of the time, we end up curling ourselves even more in the position we defend.

If you want to influence another person, you better not discuss and ignore the contrary arguments of the other person (this strategy is one used by all politicians in our country).

## 6. Extra trick: Use your voice well

The voice is a key element when it comes to influencing others.

There are four aspects of the voice to consider; these four elements, which make us perceive a certain voice differently, are; intensity, tone, timbre, and duration.

On the union of all parties, it will depend on a voice being more or less persuasive. The ideal formula to be persuasive with our voice would be like that; medium-strong intensity, serious tone, opens bell, and medium-fast duration.

# CHAPTER 2

# COGNITIVE BEHAVIORAL THERAPY

# What Is Cognitive-Behavioral Therapy?

For most of the twentieth century, psychoanalysis was the most common type of psychotherapy. Clients had to see a therapist several times a week, often for several years. In the 1970s, a large number of new forms of psychotherapy appeared; many lasted only a few weeks or months.

In 1979, Time magazine announced that there were nearly 200 types of psychotherapy. In 2010, this number would be between 400 and 500. However, a direct comparison reveals that only a few therapeutic methods are instrumental in resolving the problems for which people generally ask for help such as depression, anxiety, phobias, and stress. Increasingly, Cognitive Behavioral Therapy (CBT) is being recognized as the "standard of excellence," which is the best type of therapy for these kinds of problems, as confirmed by over 375 clinical studies since 1977 and current international treatment guidelines, based on the knowledge of experts in the field. For example, the United States National Institute of Mental Health (NIMH) and the UK National Institute for Health and Clinical Excellence (NICH) have concluded that among the various psychological treatments for anxiety and depression, CBT is the recommended first-line psychological treatment.

CBT is effective for all age groups, from infancy to senior years, regardless of educational background, income, and ethnicity. It has also proven effective in individual and group sessions.

**Introduction to CBT**

CBT is based on an intensive short-term approach (six to twenty sessions) focused on problem-solving. It is a fast, practical, and goal-oriented therapy that allows clients to develop long-term skills to stay healthy.

CBT focuses on the present moment and the problems that occur daily. It helps clients examine how they interpret and evaluate what is happening around them and the effects of this perception on their emotional experience.

CBT does not focus on childhood experiences and events. Still, these can be examined to help clients understand and deal with the emotional disorders that occurred early in life and understand the possible effects of these experiences on how they react to events.

According to CBT principles, what we feel is related to our perception of a situation and not just the nature of that situation. This idea has its origin in ancient Eastern and Western philosophies. It was incorporated into the general psychotherapeutic approach in the early 1960s. In his first work, Aaron T. Beck, the father of CBT, described the negative thought patterns associated with depression (e.g., being critical of oneself, the world, and the future). He also described ways to target and mitigate negative thoughts to improve mood. Later, Beck and his colleagues focused on the content of ideas and thought processes associated with anxiety, as well as ways to deal with anxiety problems. Since its inception, CBT has become one of the most widely used therapeutic methods.

**How is CBT happening?**

During a CBT, you learn to recognize, question, and change the thoughts, attitudes, beliefs, and superstitions related to your problematic emotional and behavioral responses in certain situations.

By taking note of your thoughts in situations that cause emotional upheaval, you learn that your thinking can aggravate emotional problems such as depression and anxiety. CBT shows you how to mitigate these problems by:

- Recognizing the distortions of your thoughts.
- Considering your thoughts as ideas of what is happening and not as facts.
- Taking a step back from your thoughts to see the situation from another angle.
- For CBT to be effective, you need to be ready to discuss your thoughts, beliefs, and behaviors and participate.

Exercises during sessions. To get the best results, you should also do the activities planned at home.

# What disorders can be treated by

# CBT?

CBT is effective in treating a wide range of psychological disorders, including:

- Mood disorders such as depression and bipolar disorder;
- Anxiety disorders, including specific phobias (e.g., fear of animals, heights, enclosed spaces), panic disorder, social phobia (social anxiety disorder), generalized anxiety, obsessive-compulsive disorder, and post-traumatic stress disorder;
- Bulimia and binge eating;
- Dysmorphophobia (body image);
- Substance use disorders (e.g., tobacco, alcohol, and other drugs).

CBT can also help people:

- Who has a psychosis;
- Tear off hair or scratch always or have tics;
- Who have sexual problems or relationship difficulties;
- Insomniacs;
- With chronic fatigue syndrome;
- Suffering from chronic pain (persistent);
- Having longstanding interpersonal issues.

In CBT, a similar method is used to treat different emotional problems. However, the method and strategies used vary and are adapted to the problem.

**Why is CBT effective?**

CBT is an effective therapeutic method because of it:

- Is structured;
- Is problem-oriented and goal-oriented;
- Teaches strategies and develops skills that have proven themselves;
- Emphasizes the importance of establishing a healthy, collaborative relationship between the therapist and the client.

To describe how CBT works, this guide will focus on using this therapy to treat people with an emotional disorder.

# Basics Of Cognitive Behavioral Therapy

Most people believe that an event or situation causes their distress: "I quarreled with my con-join this morning, and I am still angry." "My boss said he was dissatisfied with my job; I am discouraged "or" I read in the newspaper this morning that my actions had gone down. It frightens me ". In each example, the person indicates how the situation caused his emotional upheaval.

However, what you feel in a given situation depends not only on this situation but also on how you perceive it or the meaning you give it. This way of seeing your emotional reaction as being determined by what you think of a situation is one of the underlying assumptions of cognitive-behavioral therapy.

For example, a smashing noise near the window of your room wakes you up at 3 am. Your reaction to this situation will depend on what you believe to be the cause of this noise. If you think an intruder caused it, you will probably be scared and will leave the room running to make you safe. If you believe that the noise was created by the person with whom you share your apartment (if any), who came through the window because she (again!) Forgot her key, you will probably experience frustration and irritation and will react by arguing with her. Finally, if you believe that the noise was caused by your partner, who comes to see you for dating, you will probably be excited.

## Nature of automatic thoughts

In each of the previous examples, the situation is the same: a smashing noise near the window at 3 a.m. However, you might have a different quick thought to assess the situation, so-called automatic thinking in CBT. It is thought that suddenly comes to mind and determines the emotion you will feel (e.g., fear, annoyance, excitement) and the behavior that will result (p. e.g., flight, confrontation, cordial reception).

These sudden automatic thoughts influence your emotional and behavioral response more than the situation.

## Evaluation of automatic thoughts

In general, automatic thoughts are so brief and so quickly replaced by your awareness of the emotions that follow that you might not notice them.

The ability to take note of your automatic thoughts and evaluate them during a troubling situation is one of the essential skills you will develop and practice in CBT. You will also learn to ask yourself the following question: "What came to mind when I realized that I was upset? ".

**Do the following exercise.** Think about an event that has upset you today or in the past few days and has caused you anxiety, sadness, or anger. Try to remember what you were thinking at the time. By recognizing the thoughts you had in this situation, you might discover the automatic ideas that came to your mind that you were not aware of at the time.

By identifying the automatic thoughts you have had, it will be easier for you to determine the nature of the emotion that has resulted and to understand why the situation has so upset you.

**Automatic thought patterns**

In many cases, when people start to watch their automatic thoughts and take note of them, they discern a pattern. In the early CBT books he wrote in the 1960s, Aaron T. Beck found that a large number of patients who were depressed had automatic thoughts characterized by a negative perception of themselves ("I am good for nothing"). The world around them ("Nobody loves me") and the future ("I'm bad, and I will not change"). This thought pattern has been dubbed the "cognitive triad" of depression.

In the 1980s, Mr. Beck described a pattern of thoughts in tomatoes that seemed peculiar to anxiety. Clients said they had more ideas about threats and danger ("What if something terrible happened?") And the inability to adapt to a situation ("It's unbearable. Cannot continue like this").

The way a situation or event is perceived varies from person to person. However, the nature of the automatic thoughts of depressed or anxious people becomes predictable and conforms to individual characteristics.

The CBT aims, in particular, to help you become aware of

your automatic thoughts. It shows you how to step back and question, evaluate, and rectify incorrect negative automatic thoughts. However, CBT does not present positive thinking as a solution to the problems of life. This therapy is intended to teach you how to evaluate your experiences and issues in different ways (positive, negative, and neutral) so that you can draw accurate conclusions and find creative solutions to your difficulties.

## Recognition of distortions of automatic thoughts

On the other hand, the negative automatic thoughts of people with an emotional disorder are usually distorted or wrong. For example, the person who says, "I will never find a soul mate" because she had a bad experience at an appointment dramatizes the outcome of the meeting. And is more likely to experience disruption, excessive emotional that the person who says to himself, "This appointment did not go well, but I hope that the next will be better." Here is another example. A student who considers himself "stupid" and "shabby" because he had a bad grade on an exam gets a label and sees things in an all-or-nothing perspective. He is, therefore, more likely to be upset than a student who says, "I did not get the grade I wanted. I will ask for help and study more thoroughly next time."

Distortions of thought amplify the emotional importance of everyday events. CBT aims to make you more aware of your distorted perception of everyday experiences, especially when you are upset.

We all have negative automatic thoughts and cognitive distortions from time to time. However, some people are more likely to have intuitive ideas related to depression and anxiety and to have more cognitive distortions. CBT assumes that automatic thoughts are influenced by two "deeper" levels of thinking that make some people more likely to have negative and distorted views. These deeper levels are called rules and assumptions and fundamental beliefs.

## Rules and assumptions

From the beginning of childhood, you learn rules and make assumptions when interacting with family members and the world around you. For example, you may learn rules about:

- How to interact with other people (e.g., "if you have nothing good to say, do not say anything");
- Situations in which it is acceptable to express emotions (e.g., "never show your nervousness");
- Your performance (e.g., "if you cannot do something perfectly well, it's not worth trying" or "I should excel in everything I do").

You may not be aware of these rules and assumptions. However, when you begin to monitor your automatic thoughts in unexpected situations, you will be able to see the patterns of your intuitive ideas that relate to the rules you have learned and the assumptions you make.

For example, if you assume that you have to excel in everything you do, you will be more likely to be confused if you do not get an optimal result (e.g., you fail an exam, you do not receive a promotion, you are not retained for a job) than a person who does not make such an assumption.

The rules and underlying assumptions can cause automatic thoughts.

CBT aims to help you become aware of your rules and assumptions and their influence on the negative automatic thoughts you have in emotionally disturbing situations.

**Basic beliefs**

Your fundamental beliefs are at the deepest level of cognition, a level even more profound than where your rules and assumptions lie. In general, fundamental beliefs are learned early in life. They are based on rigid and absolute notions of oneself, others, and the world. Examples of positive fundamental beliefs: "I am attractive," "I am intelligent," and "People love me." Examples of negative fundamental beliefs are: "I am good for nothing," "I am weak," "People are dangerous," "I cannot trust anyone," "The world is a scary and overwhelming place."

Aaron T. Beck suggested that people with negative fundamental beliefs are more vulnerable to depression and anxiety than people with positive fundamental beliefs. Negative basic beliefs may be inactive and affect a person only when a stressful life event occurs, such as the death of a family member, a break-up, or the loss of a job. For example, a woman who believes mentally that she does not deserve to be loved can also think that if she does all she can to please her spouse, he may love her anyway. However, if her spouse leaves her, this woman may begin to believe that she does not deserve to be loved, which may make her more vulnerable to depression or anxiety.

One of the underlying assumptions of CBT is that one can learn to recognize, evaluate, and modify underlying assumptions and beliefs just as one can understand and change negative automatic thoughts. As soon as you begin to mitigate your negative assumptions and expectations, negative and distorted automatic thoughts start to diminish. The lessening of underlying negative assumptions and underlying beliefs that give rise to emotional problems alleviates emotional upheaval and partially protects against the re-emergence of depression and anxiety.

In summary, CBT differs from many other therapeutic methods in that it focuses on ways to help you determine the connection between your thoughts, feelings, and behavior. Although the latter are interdependent (they influence each other), CBT emphasizes the role of cognition (automatic ideas, rules and assumptions, and fundamental beliefs) in the appearance and maintaining emotional difficulties such as depression and anxiety.

The purpose of CBT is to help you recognize, evaluate, and modify your usual patterns of thinking for each of these levels of cognition. With the help of the therapist, you will learn that by giving a less extreme, pragmatic, and accurate sense to adverse events, your emotional and behavioral reactions will be less intense and less disturbing. Once you have developed these skills during therapy, you become your therapist and will be able to cope with painful experiences and emotional upheavals.

# CBT And Cognitive Changes

We all have automatic thoughts that spring into our minds. They can be positive, neutral, or negative. CBT is particularly interested in negative automatic thoughts related to intense moods. In the beginning, CBT aims to teach you to recognize negative automatic thoughts and cognitive distortions that occur in problematic situations. Some people develop this skill quickly while others need more time.

**Determining the links between thoughts, mood, and behavior**

To recognize the automatic thoughts and cognitive distortions that occur in problem situations, you should first talk to your CBT therapist about situations that have upset you recently. This discussion will help you discover the connection between your thoughts, mood, and behavior. Here is an example:

**Therapist:** Can you describe a situation that has troubled you in the past week?

**Pierre:** I was in the subway, and I noticed everyone who was in a relationship.

**Therapist:** What did you feel at that moment?

**Pierre:** I was sad and angry.

**Therapist:** What did you think when you were sad and angry?

**Pierre:** I told myself that everyone seems to have someone in their life except me, and that is unfair.

**Therapist:** And if it's true that everyone seems to have someone in your life except you, do you think it reveals anything about you?

**Peter:** Yeah, that I'm a shabby and that I'll always be alone.

**Therapist:** What did you do while you thought about it and had these feelings?

**Pierre:** After a while, I could not take it anymore. I got off the metro even though I had not arrived at my destination. I went home, I sat on my bed, and I thought about it all.

Here are the elements of this example:

- **Situation:** In the subway, Pierre notices the presence of couples.
- **Mood:** Sad and angry.
- **Thoughts:** "Everyone has someone in their life except me, it's unfair; I am a shabby and I will always be alone." Behavior: Pierre comes down from the subway, then goes back to the house to mull over all that.

In this example, to determine why Peter was sad and angry, we must understand what he was thinking:

- He does not have a romantic relationship, and he wants one;
- It is unfair that everyone seems to have what he wants to have;
- Because he does not have a romantic relationship now, he will never find a soul mate, and he will always be alone.

**Challenging and evaluating negative automatic thoughts**

As you learn to recognize your negative automatic thoughts, you will also learn to question and evaluate them. One of the main goals of CBT is to help you think of your dreams as ideas that do not necessarily correspond to reality. In other words, your thoughts are not necessarily truths.

To help you achieve this goal, the therapist will perform "cognitive restructuring" exercises that will teach you how to step back, question your negative self-thoughts, and evaluate the evidence that supports your thoughts and the ones that contradict them. You can then determine if your ideas are right or wrong.

In the previous example, a CBT therapist could ask Peter the following questions:

- Among the people you love and respect, is there anyone who is not in a relationship?

- Have you ever had romantic relationships?
- If one of your friends thought of you, what would you say to him?
- Can you ignore experiences you've had that suggest you will not be alone?
- Do you hold yourself responsible for something that is partly out of your control?

This approach is not intended to question Peter's thoughts, but rather to bring him to challenge the accuracy of his automatic opinions in the light of his real situation.

**Recognition and correction of cognitive distortions**

To recognize and modify the negative automatic thoughts associated with strong emotions, you must also learn to recognize the distortions or "errors" of thinking that occur when you find yourself in a troubling situation or remember such a situation.

Distortions of thinking are more likely to occur when you are troubled because emotional turmoil can undermine your strengths so that you could rely more on shortcuts or more straightforward ways of thinking. We all have distortions of thought from time to time. Here are some examples (Burns, 1999):

- **All or nothing (black or white):** Perceive things in black or white, without greyish zones (e.g., Amina got three A +, two A, and one B + during her session and believes that because she did not get only A, she failed).

- **Rejection of the positive:** Ignore positive experiences and see only the negative side (e.g., John is a dedicated father who helps his son with homework every night and spends as much time with him as possible). As he had to be absent more than usual recently because of his work, Jean thinks he is a "bad father").

- **Over-generalization:** Considering a unique experience as a continual event (e.g., Ingrid was anxious during the meeting, she concluded she would never be comfortable with her co-workers).

- **Mental filter:** Give great importance to a negative detail (e.g., Denis speaks to a group of ten young people in the church, only sees one who does not seem interested in the place of the nine others who listen carefully).

- **Dramatization:** Consider the worst, that is, assume that a situation will be more terrible or horrible than it probably will be (e.g., one morning, as Susan gets up, she notices a redness). On the back of her leg, instead of thinking of all that could have caused this redness, she immediately concludes that she has skin cancer and rushes to her doctor.

- **Reading the thought:** Quickly conclude that a person has a negative perception of you before knowing all the facts (e.g., at the movies, Guy stumbles and topples his popcorn and his drink. world must think he is a shabby man).

- **Personalization:** Believe that things are wrong and that they are the cause (e.g., Charlotte is organizing a party, she notices that two of her guests are alone and do not speak.) She begins to believe that this is his fault if they do not have fun.

**Taking note of your thoughts**

At the beginning of treatment, the CBT therapist will ask you questions to help you recognize and question your negative self-thoughts and cognitive distortions. As you make progress, the therapist will ask you to complete the thoughts book at home, in anticipation of the next session. Over time, you will become accustomed to completing this register, which will allow you to question and evaluate your automatic thoughts, as well as alleviate the emotional troubles you experience in your daily life.

It is recommended that you complete the thoughts register shortly after the end of the distressing situation or event because that is when you are most aware of the ideas generated by the experience you come from, To live. However, it is sometimes difficult to do this, for example, if you risk exposing your personal life or if the problem arises at work or at another time when it is inconvenient to complete the registration. In such a case, try to fill in the register later in the day before you forget the details. Thus, you will recover more quickly from the trouble you have experienced.

**Target assumptions and beliefs**

As the therapy progresses, the CBT therapist will introduce other cognitive strategies and home-based exercises that serve to target your assumptions and fundamental ideas.

To identify your assumptions and fundamental beliefs, you can use the register of thoughts, for it identifies situations that cause an emotional disorder and to identify the thread. The CBT therapist can help you challenge and evaluate your assumptions and beliefs and generate insights that will make it easier for you to compose when you find yourself in troubling situations.

Another way in which CBT is used to target the assumptions and beliefs that need to be changed is to write a negative fundamental understanding of yourself on a sheet of paper (e.g., "Unfriendly") and, on the backside, a less disturbing belief that you would like to have (e.g., "friendly"). You will then have to keep a record of your experiences during the week by indicating situations that seemed to confirm your positive or negative belief. In cases where you have gathered evidence to support your negative mindset, you will need to re-examine the situation carefully to identify facts that support and contradict your belief to arrive at a more balanced perspective.

**Behavioral experiences**

One of the best ways to challenge and evaluate underlying assumptions and beliefs is to test their validity with behavioral experiments. For example, if you think someone will make fun of you if you make a mistake, you might be asked to go through an analysis to determine what happens when you make a mistake. Of course, you will be asked to submit only to the experiences that you think you can do and only when you have learned ways to deal with the full range of potential outcomes that such experiences may have.

When you're ready, you might be asked to make a mistake like purse money while you line up at a store checkout or spill a drink in a cafeteria. You will be able to determine:

a) How much people notice your mistake.

b) Their reaction (e.g., they laugh and ridicule you, as you fear, or they do not seem to notice or criticize you).

c) How you deal with the situation.

In summary, the initial goal of CBT is to help you recognize and modify negative automatic thoughts that cause emotional distress in problem situations. You will learn to identify and rectify negative automatic thoughts and cognitive distortions that arouse intense moods. The thought register is the primary tool used to make cognitive changes. Other cognitive strategies, including the following, are used to reinforce the progress you make when you modify negative automatic thoughts and the assumptions and beliefs they are based on:

- Determine the advantages and disadvantages of these beliefs;
- Study the evidence that supports the assumptions and expectations and those that contradict them;
- Have a less extreme and balanced perception of oneself, others and the world;
- Submit to behavioral experiments.

# Use of CBT for Behavioral Changes

Until now, we have focused on the cognitive aspect of CBT, that is, the modification of cognitive elements, or thoughts, which can cause an emotional disorder. We will now look at behaviors that can aggravate or prolong negative moods.

Changing thinking and behavior changes go hand in hand. If you change your perception of a situation or problem, you could also improve your behavior and vice versa. If you change the way you approach a situation or problem, you may perceive it differently. For example, if you smoke and find new information that makes you think that smoking is more dangerous than you thought, you might decide to quit smoking (a cognitive change leads to a change in behavior). Or, if you stop for a week because you are sick or unable to smoke, you might say, "If I can quit smoking for a week, maybe I can do it for a month." This way of thinking may cause you to change your behavior and try to quit smoking for a month (a change in behavior leads to cognitive change).

CBT uses a variety of behavioral methods and strategies to alleviate your distress. You will find more details on this in the next pages.

**Self-monitoring**

We talked about the register of thoughts, which recognizes and evaluates negative thoughts and cognitive distortions. The registry is one of the self-monitoring techniques that you will be asked to use during CBT. You could also be asked to do the following exercises:

- Monitor your moods or feelings every day that gives you pleasure or give you the impression of being in control of a situation, for example by giving them a score ranging from zero to 10 or from zero to 100;
- Monitor the symptoms of your problem in specific circumstances;
- Plan activities or monitor the progress you have made to achieve a goal related to your behavior; for example, schedule fitness sessions for the week or record the number of times you have been training during the week.

**DAILY Self-Monitoring**

By taking note of problems every day, we become more aware of situations that may "trigger" distress. The monitoring forms used during CBT help clients recognize the type of reactions they have in stressful situations. For example, they can determine whether certain events trigger feelings such as sadness, anguish, anger, hurt, or disappointment.

The monitoring forms also allow people who fill them to be more aware of the intensity of their moods. Thus, they can determine if a situation often causes low anxiety, while another condition always causes very intense anxiety.

Finally, the monitoring forms are not just for taking note of problems. They also help people who use them to become aware of the progress they have made. For example, these forms can be used to determine the extent to which a person has achieved a behavioral goal, as well as the events and tasks performed that give him or her the feeling that she or he is in control of a situation. (sense of accomplishment and acquired skill).

In general, people who experience depression or have other emotional problems that disrupt motivation-their activities and engage in an event tend to report a lower level of pleasure than they felt while they were doing it. One way for a person to become more aware of what they are doing with their time, the comfort they have gained from their activities, and their mastery of each activity is to take note of all they have done and felt. If you have a problem with motivation, taking note of your actions can help you recognize that you are having more fun and feel more like being in control of a situation rather than doing activities than when you are doing something. In simple terms, an action, however trivial, can make you feel better.

**Self-monitoring Of Symptoms**

For almost all clinical problems treated with CBT, there are specialized forms that allow you to monitor your symptoms and take note of them during treatment. Keeping track of your experiences and taking note of them alone can improve your mood and well-being. As a result, clients are generally encouraged to do this after the first CBT session.

If you are following therapy for anxiety, you may be asked to fill out a form where you will describe your particular symptoms, depending on the anxiety problem you are experiencing. For example, if you are undergoing therapy for social anxiety, you will be asked to fill out a form where you will record distressing social situations and those where you have experienced performance anxiety in the past. If you are following therapy for an obsessive-compulsive disorder, you.

Indicate on the form the nature of the obsessive thoughts and distress they caused during the week, as well as the duration and frequency of the compulsive rituals.

**Calendar of Activities**

You can write down your schedule Which will be used to monitor your activities and give them a score based on the fun and impression of control of the situation they gave you, can also be used to program activities that you may have. Tried to avoid. This calendar can help you decide whether to go to an event or not. For example, if you choose in advance to exercise on Tuesday from 5 pm to 6 pm, you are more likely to do so than if you wait to see how you will feel that day before making a decision.

The therapist may ask you to include pleasant activities in your calendar (e.g., going out to dinner with a friend) and tasks that make you feel like you are in control (e.g., paying bills) for the next week. He will probably ask you to keep a record of the automatic thoughts that you will have as you go about your activities to help you recognize the distortions and other assessments you make that reduce the enjoyment of the activity and the activity. The impression that you are in control of the situation.

Also, the calendar of activities helps you recognize the factors that prevent you from doing specific tasks and divide these tasks into more uncomplicated actions to alleviate the distress they cause and increase the chances of you accomplished. You can define "staggered tasks" so that you will make the parts easier before performing the more difficult and complicated elements. By merely changing the structure of the tasks to be completed and the process you are following, you can significantly increase the chances of accomplishing these tasks.

**Exhibition therapy**

Exposure therapy is an integral part of CBT in the treatment of anxiety. It aims to reduce the fear of certain things (e.g., insects, snakes) or specific situations (e.g., confined spaces, heights) by gradually increasing exposure to these things or in these situations. To start, you may be asked to think about the idea or situation that scares you or to look at an image that illustrates it (indirect exposure) and expose yourself to it more and more until you can touch this thing or put you in this situation (direct exposure).

By gradually exposing yourself to your fears, your anguish will diminish, and you will learn that your concerns are excessive and irrational. This process is called habituation (or exhaustion of effect).

In general, exposure therapy begins with exposure to situations that elicit mild to moderate fear. The client is then gradually exposed to conditions that create more intense fear. Before starting this therapy, you should rank your concerns in ascending order and indicate all the situations that are causing you anxiety as well as the levels of anxiety associated with each trigger.

At first, the therapist will help you expose yourself to your fears, and as you progress, you will have to expose yourself to it after the sessions. Your progress will depend on the intensity of your fear and your ability to withstand the discomfort associated with your anxiety. You must expose yourself to your fear several times and long enough (usually at least 30 minutes) to get the best results possible. You will learn that your anxiety naturally decreases when you are long enough in the situation that causes fear.

**Behavioral experiences**

The behavioral experiences described previously allowed you to analyze your assumptions and beliefs. Through these experiences, you will be exposed to a scary situation to determine if your fears will come true. If the result that scares you occurs, the experiments will also allow you to learn how well you have coped with the situation.

Experiences are behavioral because they force you to "try" new ways of thinking by changing your habits, usually by putting yourself in specific situations and choosing a different behavioral strategy.

# CHAPTER 3

# NEURO-LINGUISTIC PROGRAMMING?

# What Is It And How Does It Work?

Neuro-linguistic programming helps us to change behavior patterns and thoughts even very traumatic or rooted in ourselves. In this chapter, we reveal some of the NLP techniques that will help you achieve it.

Richard Bandler and John Grinder created the neurolinguistic programming (NLP) in California (United States) in the seventies. Its creators affirm that there is a connection between neurological procedures, language, and behavioral patterns learned.

The creators of the NLP took three teachers, Fritz Perls, Virginia Satir, and Milton Erickson, and through various studies, they verified that these three people possessed special communication skills that allowed them to obtain excellent results with their patients. That way, they were creating a set of tools that they later called neurolinguistic programming.

"NLP is like the nuclear physics of the mind. Physics studies the structure of reality, the nature of the world. NLP does the same with its brain. It allows decomposing the phenomena in the constituent parts that determine their operation."

**(Tony Robbins)**

## The elements of neurolinguistic programming

It has happened to all of us that we react to a situation, and then our inner voice tells us that we should have said something else or reacted in another way. Actually, our way of responding and thinking is conditioned by a neurological map that encodes and stores our way of responding to a situation.

That map is made up of our past, our present, and our future. And from it, we build our beliefs, lessons, and behaviors learned.

The structures of our mind are so strongly rooted in us that we cannot influence them, at least in a conscious way. The mind works on two levels: conscious (logical thinking) and unconscious (automatic functioning).

## The neurolinguistic programming and conscious and unconscious mind

The conscious mind is the always alert one, which allows us to remember dates and names of people, for example. And the unconscious mind is one that activates all behaviors, beliefs, values , etc. that we have learned and that shape our way of acting. It is not always consciously accessible. And, for example, it is what allows us to drive, write an email, or open a window.

For our unconscious mind to "draw" a new map, it has to act with a clear objective that answers the question, what do we want? And the complicated thing is precisely that, that on many occasions we do not know what we want. Therefore, we do not know how to define our objective.

For this, we have to think of something that changes our habitual behavior in a situation, something that is apparently impossible.

### The objectives in NLP

The purposes that we propose in the neurolinguistic programming sessions must answer a series of questions. The result is to achieve a significant change in our behavior.

### Is it a positive goal?

For our programming to work, we must define a positive objective. Our goal cannot begin with, "I don't want that ...". It's about highlighting what you want to achieve, not what you want to avoid.

### Does it benefit you?

Your goal should be something you do for yourself, and that depends on yourself, not on others. For example, it is very common that the goal of young people is to finish a university career, but that is not a goal of them but of their parents. You must also control what you do to reach your goal so that it depends on you. We cannot wish as a goal to make good weather on the weekend, because it is not up to us.

### How will you know that you are reaching them?

Think about what you will be doing at that moment and how you will feel. Visualize each action, each feeling that this moment provokes, how it smells, what flavor you feel, what you hear, how you move, what you do. In addition to knowing if we are achieving our objective, we will have to set ourselves goals in the short term and measure their fulfillment. For example, if my goal is to find work, a goal will have to be to look for job offers and offers each week.

**Is your goal specific?**

You must make clear what you want and what you don't. The more defined and detailed your objective is, the easier it will be to establish the steps to achieve it. For example, if we define the objective, "I want to find a job," it is a very generic objective.

But, if we redefine the objective by giving details, we will have much clearer goals to achieve our objective. For example: "From February 1, 2020, I will work in a company dedicated to computer science that will pay me 2000 euros a month."

**What resources do you need to make it happen?**

Think about the resources you already have and those you need broadly: knowledge, objects, financial resources, help from third parties.

Once our goal is set, we must review our beliefs and values. What we have deeply rooted in ourselves and that prevents us from reaching our dreams. We must change the negative belief structures that make us impede to go towards our goal.

**What prevents me from achieving my goal?**

One of the biggest obstacles we will encounter on the road to our dreams is the opinions of others. Remember that each person has different perspectives, and we must put ourselves in their place to try to understand their reasoning.

All the way to go towards your goal, visualize your dream, feel how it smells, what is heard, what you touch, and especially the feeling and feeling of happiness that causes you to achieve your goal. And reach your dream! Turn your aspiration into reality!

Finally, for our subconscious mind to learn a new program that allows us to realize our dream, it must perceive the reason, the reason.

In NLP, the learning process is established in four phases:

- **Phase 1:** Unconscious Incompetence. I don't know I don't know.
- **Phase 2:** Conscious Incompetence. I know I don't know.
- **Phase 3:** Conscious competition. I know I know.
- **Phase 4:** Unconscious competition. I don't know what I know.

To unlearn, we go from step 4 to 2 and to relearn from step 2 to 4. Once we have learned the new program, we can apply it at the moment it is necessary. Therefore, NLP helps us create new mental programs that facilitate many aspects of our lives and help us work on goals to achieve what we dream and desire.

The most significant development of NLP has occurred in interpersonal relationships and the workplace. In both areas, you can use NLP to train your skills, overcome obstacles, resolve conflicts, and influence other people.

In conclusion, NLP gives you the necessary tools to control how to respond to your environment, how to perceive it, and thus take steps to make your dreams come true.

# The principles of NLP

## 1. The inner card is unique

One of the principles of NLP relates to the orientation of the people in the world around them. The direction of the person has to do with the inner card. In the early stages of life, the inner card is simple. As we grow, however, the map becomes more complex, and new paths open.

## 2. The best map offers more than one road

As mentioned in the previous point, the complete map is also more accurate and offers more options to reach a goal or solve the problem. This is related to flexibility and the ability to respond to a vital event in a number of ways. The map is not the area that represents it, but if it is correct, it has a similar structure to the area and is more useful.

## 3. Every behavior has a positive intention

This can be one of the most discussed principles of NLP. This point refers to the fact that every person and every action has an intrinsic property positive intent. For example, someone may doubt that a smoker has a positive intention to smoke. However, according to this principle, the smoker may smoke to relax or be socially accepted. NLP tries to redirect this positive intention towards a more adaptable behavioral pattern and suitable for the person.

## 4. The structure of the experience

This principle shows how each experience is composed of a particular structure. Every thought, every feeling, every memory, or experience It consists of a series of elements. This means that if every experience has a structure, its effect can be changed thanks to a change in composition.

## 5. All problems have a solution

This principle refers to the fact that all problems have a solution. It may seem perfect because sometimes certain solutions can not be carried out. At other times, there will be problems that do not have a clear solution. This has to do with the card the person has The fewer roads or alternatives you have, the fewer solutions you can give to the specific situation. Also, the interpretation of the problem has to do with the content of the map. A richer map that offers more resources will find certain situations less of a problem.

## 6. Everyone has the strength he needs

This is one of the principles of NLP, which has to do with the personal development of the person, as they are referred to. Everyone has the necessary strength to achieve what is suggested. The problem arises when a person's limiting beliefs influence self-esteem.

## 7. Body and mind are part of the same system

This principle refers to Man is body and mind. In other words, every emotion and emotion affects the body. This also applies vice versa. For example, a disease that affects the body has psychological effects. Therefore, for NLP, the thought changes that alter physical issues are important. By the way, did you already hear of that? Embodied knowledge?

## 8. The importance of communication depends on the result

It is necessary to establish clear communication guidelines that do not lead to misunderstandings nor an option for biased personal interpretations by the recipient of the message.

## 9. There are no failures, but opportunities

When a person moves continuously, they have different ways to reach the goal. The failures must be seen as opportunities, that is, as measures that you can overcome and move in the desired direction.

## 10. If something does not work, try something else

Sometimes people insist on doing something that does not work, nor do they change the way they act. At this point, the famous phrase "do not expect different results if you always do the same thing" makes sense. NLP Practitioners Want to Help Recognize and modify these behaviors that are not effective and keep repeating with the same stone.

# Three keys to NLP to change your life

The keys to NLP (neuro-linguistic programming) can be incredibly useful in changing the way we perceive and interpret reality. We cannot forget that our thoughts and feelings shape everything that surrounds us. Hence the techniques that accompany this approach are useful for us to become aware of it and apply appropriate changes.

In one way or another, we have all heard about neurolinguistic programming. More than psychological theory, we should see it instead as a set of personal development strategies. With them, what their creators, Richard Bandler and John Grinder, were looking for back in the 70s, was to model the abilities of the human being to allow him to achieve his vital purposes by himself.

On the other hand, it should be noted that there is no lack of critical voices regarding this model, who distrusts NLP, seeing it instead as a type of pseudoscience. Now, it should be said that their strategies turn out to be quite useful in many cases, as well as impressive from the psychological point of view. Thus, one of its main objectives is to establish a connection between neurological processes, our language, and behavioral patterns learned through experience.

Thus, by correcting our cognitive representations and removing power from those rigid mental maps that sometimes characterize us, we gradually shape much more adaptive behavior patterns. The keys to NLP are an exciting and useful way to change our reality, to model our mind, our way of feeling what surrounds us to perceive life in a freer, more positive, happy way.

These would be three strategies to achieve it.

## 1. Dissociation technique

NLP or neurolinguistic programming explains that our lack of confidence, as well as anxiety or stress, are activities, processes, not permanent conditions. The key is, therefore, to control these processes, change them so that they flow in a more appropriate direction and of course, in our favor.

One way to achieve this is through dissociation. The steps would be as follows:

- Identify that emotion that you want to stop, that you want to calm and dissolve from your mind, such as anger, anger, fear, disappointment...
- What we must do is focus on that particular emotion and on a situation that provokes it regularly. For example, I feel anger every time my co-worker speaks behind my back.
- We will visualize that scene as if it were a movie, and what we will do with it is the following: we will provide it with a fun soundtrack to remove drama. Then, we will reproduce it more times in our mind to reduce negative emotions, to perceive that

everything is under our control and that this situation, far from affecting us, is already unimportant; It can even prove ironic. The rage has disappeared.

## 2. Re-frame content

Another of the keys to NLP may be evident to any of us, but it is no less accurate that we tend to forget it or not know how to combine it properly. If we become obsessed with anticipating fatalities, in facing our day to day with fear and always thinking the worst, it is possible that in the end, we will generate our death.

For example, some keep thinking about what would happen to him or her if their partner left him if he betrayed him. Their anguish is such that they end up developing obsessive behaviors, jealousy, distrust, and a whole range of harmful processes that end up crystallizing in their worst fear: the couple ends up leaving them for not supporting that situation anymore.

Thus, one way to control these fears is to make use of content re-framing. It is based on a cognitive technique were to shift attention focused on fear to frame it in other more constructive aspects.

For example, I must stop focusing on the fear of losing my partner to focus on building good times by his side.

I shift my fear of being alone to focus on an essential process: taking responsibility for myself. I must learn to love myself enough, learn to be active instead of letting myself be trapped by fear.

## 3. NLP keys: the anchoring technique

The anchoring technique is undoubtedly one of the keys of the NLP most representative of this psychotherapeutic strategy of personal growth. It is based on something very concrete: an anchor is a connection between a stimulus and an emotional state. Our purpose is to achieve an adequate mood as well as dominant with which to perform a specific task or face a given situation successfully.

«Every time you are doing the same as most, it is time to Stop and Reflect.»

**-Mark Twain-**

For example, let's think about those situations that are characterized by generating anxiety or insecurity: exams, speaking in public, approaching that person that attracts us so much. If we can evoke, to put into operation a particular mental state, we will find enough momentum and security to get out (and successfully) of these very ordinary moments. These would be a few simple steps to achieve an anchor based on the NLP keys:

- We will first identify what we want to feel: trust, happiness, tranquillity...

- Now we will try to remember a moment in our life when we feel those positive emotions with high intensity.
- Focus on that memory and "trim" that image, make it yours, keep it alive.
- Now we must choose a phrase that serves as an anchor, "I am at peace" or "serenity," or "everything will be fine"...
- The strategy is to repeat this sequence (desired emotion, memory, visualization, anchor word) daily until it is integrated into our mind. In this way, the anchor will be automated little by little every time we need it.

We are sure that these keys to NLP will have aroused the curiosity of more than one in that broad and always suggestive universe that is neurolinguistic programming. If so, it is possible to say that it is an approach that is within our reach, it is part of the movement that emphasizes our enormous potential as human beings, initiated in the 70s, and that has been consolidating over the years.

# The 8 Transformative Strategies of NLP

You may have heard on occasion about NLP or Neurolinguistic Programming as a practice of personal development or excellence, and so it is. A more exact definition would be, a set of techniques aimed at analyzing, coding and modifying beliefs and behaviors through the study of language, both verbal and gestural and corporal. Today we are going to discover the transformative strategies of NLP and why it is so successful.

It is called "programming" because it is an action plan or set of operations that seek a specific objective," neuro " because it studies the processes that occur in the same nervous system and "linguistic" because we use the language (verbal and not verbal).

Do you want to know more about Neurolinguistic Programming? In this section, we explain what it is and the eight transformative strategies of NLP that are used to seek success, quality of life, or overcoming traumas and phobias.

"The brain is not a vessel to fill, but a lamp to light."

**-Plutarch-**

**The NLP method**

NLP has occupied a prominent place among the disciplines that assist in the achievement of objectives so that many psychologists, doctors, and coaches apply it in the field of personal development individually or in groups.

One of the foundations of NLP is the evidence that each of us builds different representations of reality to which we add our emotions and language processes.

By modifying our beliefs and emotions, our way of expressing ourselves, we can also change the perception of reality and the self-image we have of ourselves.

On the other hand, Neurolinguistic Programming ensures that memory and imagination use the same neurological circuits and thus have the same impact on the human being. Then, eight transformative strategies of NLP collected by psychologist Jazmín Zambrano in his book NLP for all.

## 1. Submodalities or learning styles

Submodalities are variants of representation systems, that is, in the way in which our brain encodes and classifies an experience. There are three types:

- Visual (color, distance, depth, clarity, contrast, and luminosity).
- Auditory (volume, tone, rhythm, and pauses).
- Kinesthetic (temperature, vibration, texture, pressure, movement, and weight).

All these nuances would help us, through imagination, to be able to change the characteristics of the memories we have edited as a film of our life and thus modify, for example, the memory of an unhappy childhood.

Another way to apply them would be through "dissociation." We move to the moment in which we live an unpleasant experience; we feel the touch that an object had or see what was happening, and then dissociate ourselves, leave the situation and look at it as if we were outside it, observing ourselves.

For NLP, the objective of dissociating is to remove the emotional power from the experience we have experienced. Thus, the experience loses strength, detaches itself from suffering, and can even be associated with a pleasant moment.

## 2. Anchoring technique

In the process of the anchoring technique, an external stimulus or "anchor" is associated with a positive behavior that one wishes to acquire. Anchors can be words, gestures, smells, or colors that transport us to a positive state of mind.

An example of this anchorage would be to associate the gesture of touching the ear with feeling good so that, in moments of crisis or difficulties, with that small gesture, we could recover well-being and feel better.

### 3. Reframe

The reframing, in NLP, consists of modifying the frame of reference in which a person lives the situation to change its meaning. Therefore, the emotional state and the behavior that accompanied it in principle. It is to see the glass half full instead of half empty, find an unexpected edge in the situation that manages to reverse its impact and positivize it.

### 4. Calibration

This strategy is to recognize the mental state of the individual through his verbal behavior and nonverbal, that is, if you are sad, angry, or even lying. Looking at their behavior, we can get to know each other better and help them in their process of change.

### 5. Modeling

With the modeling, it is possible to determine how other people acted to achieve success in some area of their life and to imitate them. With the modeling technique, what is attempted is the creation of representation as faithful as possible of another person, especially their behaviors to achieve something.

### 6. Induction

With the technique of induction, people are guided to certain emotional states to modify painful situations. Either induce feelings of discomfort that match the experience they had or pleasant feelings to address their fears and concerns about these situations.

## 7. Synchronization

The synchronization would be like a deep empathy, through which the feelings of others are understood until creating a strong link between the conscious and unconscious level of the interlocutor. This technique serves to optimize interpersonal communications.

## 8. Relaxation

Finally, NLP considers relaxation an effective tool to relieve tensions, expand awareness, and free the spirit. Relaxing is always good to face our day today.

## The effectiveness of NLP transformative strategies

The positive thing about the transformative strategy of NLP is that they enjoy great efficiency. Therefore, this type of therapy is so used today. It is important to mention that the strategies mentioned above will not be applied as a whole in all cases. What does this mean? That the incidence will depend on the professional in some more than in others.

With these strategies, NLP pursues a personal transformation that raises self-esteem, increases creative capacity, and helps us express ourselves more satisfactorily by improving relationships with others. Have you ever tried Neurolinguistic Programming?

# How to Manage Your Emotions through NLP

Act as if you were already the person you would like to be, and allow your emotions to be the force that drives your engine of change. You are the architect of your reality.

It is possible that you have already heard about NLP (neurolinguistic programming), and that you even have your own coach, or that for now, it is only a trend that attracts your interest but in which you have not yet deepened enough.

As curiosity is often said to be the first step towards knowledge, and if there is a powerful dimension in which we should always be up to date, it is in emotional management.

Neuro-linguistic programming (NLP) is a method that is at the service of Emotional Intelligence through a set of systems to understand and program our behavior. It teaches us to act, to deploy strategies and, above all, to manage.

Because managing is being able to face the problems in our social relationships, learn to make more effective and successful personal decisions.

**NLP and our internal programs**

We will begin by defining briefly what are the basic postulates of the NLP to have a basic guidance guide:

- Neuro-linguistic programming is a communication, personal development, and psychotherapy strategy created in the 70s.

- All our behavior is a set of habits and actions acquired by all our experiences: they are programming. An example?

In our childhood, they never recognized everything we did well; we only received sanctions, criticisms, and rejections. All this developed in us a sense of helplessness and little confidence in ourselves.

As the years have passed, our "internal programming" has been feeding even more with this feeling.

- We have thus established a connection between neurological processes ("neuro"), our language ("linguistic"), and behavioral patterns learned through experience.

People think, feel, and act according to internal programs. NLP offers us a series of appropriate tools to allow us to change, and at the same time, improve all these processes. It is a model of human experience and communication.

**NLP bases for emotional management**

We will start by telling you that NLP is very useful to complement it with our Emotional Intelligence.

Sometimes, despite knowing, we do not know how to put it into practice, so, for example, it is possible that despite knowing what are the basic pillars of EI, in your day to day, you do not know how to reproduce them:

NLP seeks to model and reproduce competent skills based on emotional intelligence so that we find success and happiness in everyday life.

Emotional Intelligence will be the speaker that will help us communicate, and NLP, for its part, will provide us with practical strategies, through continuous interaction, or "programming," between our nervous system (our "hardware"), and our language, (our "software").

**1. When our programming is based on negative emotions**

Depressions, states of depression or helplessness, are very common in our day to day. First of all, we have to refocus our ideas on them:

Negative emotions such as sadness, grief, or grief, are not eternal diseases, nor should we resign ourselves to them. It is necessary to manage them to promote CHANGE.

- Do not be afraid of them; do not fear sadness. NLP invites us to know how to administer and accept them so that they are an effective tool. For what reason? Because they are part of ourselves and of a knowledge from which we must understand their origin.

- NLP does not seek to eliminate anything in you. Pain cannot be erased, but we can understand it to offer us teaching, and teaching is a weapon of power.

Why do I feel so downcast? I don't feel well in my work situation. My work generates frustration. What does this frustration tell me? What should I make any changes, maybe? What strategies should I deploy to promote it and find myself better?

- Managing emotions mean making the most of them, making them go from being "negative" to "harmless."

## 2. Action keys to generate change

- Be aware of your emotions by listening to your body: welcome the emotions and accept them.
- Describe each emotion with words, define them aloud. Name the feeling.
- How is that feeling? Is it healthy or immobilizes you?
- Connect with your own inner strength to transform the unhealthy emotion, or those destructive thoughts into useful dimensions: make your voice act as healing.

NLP requires practice and above all, well and full awareness of our emotions. It is a daily adventure that is worth exercising to get to know each other better and bring about changes.

# The Power Of The Mind

We have heard of them, but what are NLP techniques? Indeed, we cannot talk about Neuro-linguistic Programming as a science; hence, it has received some criticism. But it is considered a "model," that is, a set of techniques and theories focused on understanding behaviors and orienting the human being towards self-knowledge and the achievement of objectives.

**But we better analyze its acronyms first:**

On the one hand, we have the word "programming," which refers to the intention to reprogram behaviors, beliefs, and psychological processes. The "neuro" concept leads us to the idea that all behavior is based on a series of neurological processes. And finally, "linguistic" responds to the concept that all these neurological processes are expressed through a specific verbal and body language.

«NLP is a set of models, skills, and techniques to think and act effectively in the world. The purpose of NLP is to be useful, increase options, and improve the quality of life.»

**-John Grinder-**

**Principles and techniques NLP**

That dimensional triad that we mentioned has as an initial objective to understand our internal processes to reprogram the way of communicating and expressing ourselves, in order to change beliefs and make us feel safe to achieve our personal success. A challenge, right? But let us know, in a brief way, some more of its aspects and NLP techniques.

## 1. The communication

NLP tells us that the way we communicate and the words we use define our reality and the way we understand the world, a personal perspective that sometimes does not match that of our interlocutors.

In addition to this, people have two types of communication: internal (what we think and feel in our internal jurisdiction) and external (where in addition to the words we speak out loud, gestures, postures, and gestures come together).

## 2. How to process information

People differ in our way by "capturing" the information. Some people are guided more by the visual, others by the auditory route, others by the sensations. Stop for a moment in this idea: How do you remember things more, with words or with images?

Try to remember a moment of your past; how does that memory come to mind? See how you analyze and capture the information around you, if you are, for example, more visual or auditory.

## 3. The anchor

One way in which to achieve objectives or overcome certain problems would be based on this concept, already used by behavioral psychology and one of the basic NLP techniques.

Imagine a situation that causes us a lot of anguish and anxiety, public speaking, for example. One way to face this reality would be to "anchor" a pleasant, relaxed, and positive moment of our memory, and associate it with visualization and breathing techniques to the "stressful situation."

A walk on the beach when we were children, a sunset with our partner, relaxing music... all this should help us "weaken that fear" and reprogram new realities where harmony prevails. In this way, gradually, we "anchor" in a quiet and pleasant situation to face an event that is stressful for us.

## 4. The weather

Time has a certain importance for each person, but you must know how to manage it properly. In the past, our memories and emotions come together, a trunk from which good things can sometimes be taken to redirect the "now."

Because it is in the present where sensory experiences prevail, in which the significant events occur and where we must invest all our efforts in view of a good future. Thus, working in the present is essential in NLP to sow the future we would like to have.

The future does not exist yet; hence, it must be established as that point where to place our desires to push our present. Ours now.

**5. Systems ecology**

People have a system of beliefs and determined values built throughout our lives, which are those engines that guide our neurological axes. "We are what we believe," and beliefs are the conceptions of our world, which promote action and behavior.

Sometimes, these beliefs are so ingrained in our being that we do not even realize if they are beneficial to us or not, we may be hurting ourselves without knowing it... Hence, NLP delves into our systems ecology to make us aware and reorganize these structures more beneficially and optimally.

"The greatest wisdom that exists is to know oneself."

**-Galileo-**

These are, then, with great strokes, the basic pillars on which this approach of the human mind is based, the Neurolinguistic Programming, where how we interpret our reality and organize the information:

The senses, the language, the time, words, memories, beliefs... are those leaves that make up the tree of our life.

NLP techniques help to vary or focus differently on any of these parts to direct our lives towards certain goals.

# Why is NLP so successful?

## NLP are methods

NLP is not a universal, universally applicable method. NLP transforms into something that everyone needs right now. The main focus of the NLP is on the uniqueness of the people. Therefore, every method is tuned to the individual. The application of NLP is always based on the analysis of the individual. Only when you know how you or your counterpart is ticking can you use NLP successfully. Knowing to solve a problem, it is important to understand how the problem works. And this is where NLP comes in. The NLP not only looks at what people think and do. The main focus is on how they think. The thought process, the subjective mental process, is considered. NLP helps us to understand this structure of subjectivity. Through this analysis of the individual, you can find out what makes a person successful or how a problem works. When you understand that, suddenly, it's easy to solve a problem or help translate success into another area of life or another person.

Albert Einstein is said to have said the phrase, "The definition of insanity is always the same to do and expect different results." In the spirit of Einstein, an important principle in the NLP is: "If what you do does not work, try something else..." Hence the claim to work on one thing for as long as the desired outcome established. NLP is flexible and flexible; it adapts to the individual and is, therefore, surprisingly successful.

## NLP is a model

NLP is a model of mental processes. A model is, by definition, not the reality but a simplified representation of reality. A model is right to the extent that it allows predictions of real events. One such example is the atomic model. This model of the atom does not pretend to explain reality altogether one hundred percent but offers a critical approach that allows statements about the behavior of atoms and molecules. It even will enable schoolchildren to make accurate statements about the behavior of particles, although the underlying reality is much more complicated. In this sense, NLP does not explain how the brain works but provides a clear idea of the processes of our psyche. As such, NLP provides a critical approach to seemingly inexplicable processes. NLP's model allows us to make changes in our mental processes, which are reflected in changes in real trade. It makes it possible, for example, to change out-of-the-way behaviors and finally implement what we set out to do.

## Is NLP dangerous?

We all agree: a sharp knife in the hands of children can be very dangerous. If you use it for cutting bread, it is a useful everyday item. In a surgeon's side, a scalpel can even be a lifesaver. So it is with the model of NLP. Learn NLP to see who is using it and how to protect yourself from negative influences if necessary.

# Ways to control anger using neuro-linguistic programming

The method of controlling the anger that I will tell you this time is highly effective. When you're on fire with an angry fire, people don't have good judgment.

In particular, thinking becomes a source of anger, will the words that were full of endlessly anger continued tour came in from the inside of your head.

In such a case, it is necessary to urgently wake up the fire of anger and instantly awaken a philosophical thought. An image is indispensable for that.

If thoughts dominate you, your head will be contaminated with negative words, and you can see the current situation only from a subjective perspective.

On the other hand, if you use the image, you will be able to view the current situation objectively.

If you can only judge the current situation from your point of view, everything else will be distorted. By making full use of the image, the current situation can be objectively recognized, so it becomes possible to separate emotions and think calmly.

## 1. Rehearsal with image

It is recommended that you first rehearse with an image to control anger. It is a method called dissociation of a technique called neuro-linguistic programming.

Imagine a movie theatre in your head. Then, imagine how you will deal with anger and your ideals.

For example, consider the case where you feel angry with your boss about your poor treatment. In a movie theatre in the headquarters, a dissociate is to imagine the situation where the boss will improve the treatment by telling the boss about the current situation.

By looking at the image in the movie theatre in your head, you will be able to image your actions objectively. By looking at the image repeatedly, it is possible to act in the actual production with the same emotion as the image.

At the same time, like a movie soundtrack If you hear the voice, "If it is, then it will be more effective."

In this example, "If you can analyze your situation accurately without telling your boss about the situation, you will be able to improve your situation."

In neuro-linguistic programming, we associate the experience of the image world with associates, and the creation of a movie theatre in the image world to see the screenings is separated from associates.

Dissociates have the effect of thinking separately from emotions, so they are often used when it is difficult to remain calm, such as anger.

## 2. Relax with an image

There is a visualization that uses an image as an anger control method that lets you let go of anger without spending time. Imagine a sight where you can relax and enjoy the sight, and your body and mind will be healed in a short time.

I introduced the method of dissociating neuro-language programming. Disassociate was a way of looking at the cinema screening film in the image. It was a way to separate and think about your anger and the situation by having an objective experience like watching a movie instead of subjective experience in the image.

In contrast, immersion in the world of images is called an associate in terms of neuro-linguistic programming. This method allows you to feel the image world more subjectively by immersing yourself in the image world.

It is not recommended to image big emotions such as anger as an associate because the energy of anger is amplified. Still, it is recommended because you can enter the world of images more if you are in a relaxing sight.

Imagine a place or sight where you can relax the most. Thinking for about 2 minutes will calm your emotions to some extent. The first priority for anger control is to control emotions. For this reason, the relaxation method using images is inseparable as a method of controlling anger.

# CHAPTER 4

# MENTAL MODELS

# What is the mental model?

Mental models are thinking devices through which a human being tries to explain to himself and others how the real world works.

It is a kind of internal symbol of hypothetical external reality representation that plays an important role in cognition — that is, in the way we grasp the world. It is the mental models of each of us that define how we perceive what happens around us, how each event will affect us, how we will think, and how we will act. Each person has their own mental model, which is the result of all their experiences, life history, and situations.

In short: the mental model can be described as a broad view of the world gained through past experiences. They are assumptions, generalizations, or even ingrained images that influence the way we see the world and act.

# What are the sources of mental models?

Each one's mental models are created primarily from four main sources: the nervous system, language, culture, and personal history.

Check below how the construction of each of them happens.

**Nervous system**

Also known as a biological filter, it concerns certain limitations as well as the physiological and cognitive abilities that each human being has.

For example, a colorblind person will not have the same interpretation of painting as one who can recognize all the colors of the landscape.

Similarly, comparing human characteristics with that of some animals would also be uneven for us and offer different experiences on both sides.

While man's ear has a limit of vibrations to be heard per minute, something close to 20,000, dogs can hear much louder sounds than we do.

Human night vision also cannot compare with that of a bat or even a cat. Our visual range is infinitely less than that of an eagle.

This impacts the way these living things act.

A shrill whistle may be hurting your dog's hearing aid while you may be hearing almost nothing.

**Personal story**

We all have a past and carry information over the years.

This baggage of ours in one way or another interferes with our mental models more or less directly, depending on the case.

Elements such as race, sexual orientation, family history, economic status, educational background, parent-teacher relationship, and other variables affect our decisions.

Some behaviors that you may be perceived as obvious, logical, and natural to others may be viewed as unreasonable and purposeless.

This is because creation and past and assimilated values are different from person to person.

Even at the beginning of our childhood, when we do not even have the critical capacity for reflection, information is incorporated into our way of being.

The examples of this mental model filter are numerous.

Imagine a sporting event that has as commentator a former athlete of the sport and a specialized journalist who studied all the theoretical part of the game.

The opinions will be different, as the former athlete tends to go to the practical side, based on his personal experience, having worked in the role. He will bring cases of the profession, situations experienced by him.

On the other hand, the journalist will weigh in on the technical side and the information he has studied and analyzed as one who critically evaluates the sport.

And this happens not only in the professional field but also in the personal.

How many people do not deprive themselves of certain experiences because they have had a bad history in some specific situation?

The important thing is to understand that this filter is about personal history. That is, the present and the future will be impacted by these experiments of yore.

It's up to everyone to deal with their trauma and memories as best they can so as not to fall into an endless looping loop that keeps them from moving on.

**Culture**

In a way, it is very similar to the previous source of mental models.

The difference is that this kind of thinking pattern, let's call it that, is influenced by the collective imagination and not by the individual.

That is, your view of the reality around you is impacted by the culture you have been subjected to or submitted to throughout your life.

And don't fall into that mistake of believing that your culture is superior to the other. That does not exist.

Western civilizations have different customs from the eastern people, for example, but that does not mean that one is better than the other.

For example, some Arab Muslim countries argue that a man can marry more than one wife.

Can you disagree with the way other people view this marriage issue? Of course, you can.

Your customs and personal experience will make you question these values.

It is wrong to be prejudiced with a tradition that is not yours and which you certainly do not fully understand.

As the only filter of mental models of a collective nature, culture can be viewed in two very different ways.

If, on the one hand, it is positive, as it helps maintain order and structure a way of thinking that extends to large numbers of people, on the other, it tends to be limiting and conservative.

Even so, cultural, mental models are the most difficult to transform and adapt to new realities.

# The origin of mental models

As we have seen, our mental models emerge long before we were born.

Culturally speaking, its origin points to hundreds or even thousands of years before us.

But over time, our biological limitations, our personal history, and our appropriation for different types of language guide the way we think and act.

It is from this combination of factors that we assemble and firm our opinions.

More important than knowing the origin of these mental models is trying to take the reins on them.

Not getting carried away by the automatism of preconceived concepts is the main challenge of the routine.

After all, it's not because you've always understood a subject in a certain way that you need to go on like this.

# Mental models that block creativity

"I can't do it." "I can't do it." "I won't even try because it won't work."

These are typical phrases that we repeat in difficult situations that require going beyond the ordinary.

But maybe it's time for you to rethink using each one.

The human unconscious sometimes imposes barriers to our actions.

It is the so-called limiting thoughts that make us fear new and different experiences.

It is that thinking that only leads to commonplace and prevents something creative from being externalized.

You know those traditional phrases, cliches like "every politician is a thief" or "blonde is dumb"?

The tip here is to put such expressions aside, and allow yourself to go further, understand the meaning behind each story and not just repeat what most propagate as truth.

# Cognitive Psychological Foundations of (Misery) Understanding

What does it take for the subjective feeling to come to understand someone or a situation? What must be the case that something is understood well enough to serve as a basis for decision-making, planning, and solving problems? And what, conversely, is the basis for potential misunderstandings and wrongdoing?

In the following section, two theoretical positions in cognitive psychology are first presented - Understanding Propositions and Understanding about Mental Models -, in which the relevance of mental models for the understanding of linguistic utterances is discussed in more detail.

A special case of mental models that is important for the processes of understanding are metaphors, which, in contrast to other linguistic forms of knowledge representation, are also closely linked to pictorial thinking. Based on investigations in the company environment, it is explained, which functions metaphors for processes of the understanding and misunderstanding in the context of knowledge cooperation and knowledge exchange in enterprises and organizations can have.

# The propositional model of (mis) understanding

Cognitive psychology knows different models with which it tries to explain the processes of understanding and misunderstanding. On the one hand, the understanding of texts and statements can be understood as the understanding of individual semantic units. In this so-called propositional representation of knowledge structures, statements based on predicate logic are presented as relations between arguments and objects.

Thus, the sentence The Greeks loved beautiful works of art as a relation with the predicate 'loved', the argument 'Greeks', and the object 'works of art' represent. This proposition represents a unity of meaning and represents the fact that Greeks loved works of art. Conjunctions can also be established between different propositional representations of this kind if different propositions have common arguments or if propositions act as arguments of other propositions. With this suggestive form of presentation, entire texts can be structurally broken down and described as a sequence of partly nested propositions. An elaborate model of propositional text processing was developed by Kintsch and van Dijk (1978), who assume that a text is processed in several cycles due to the limited cognitive processing time. By understanding and processing individual propositions separately, until finally, the understanding of the own propositions leads to an understanding of the entire text.

In the propositional model, understanding is understood as a juxtaposition of semantic entities. Understanding is possible if, as in the case of a puzzle, a given set of particles (semantic units) can be put together in such a way that a complete structure is created. Missing particles must be supplemented by the formation of so-called inferences. This understanding of understanding can be described as additive-elementary.

However, that understanding can not only proceed in this additive way was shown by various experiments. If understanding were to be based exclusively on the original propositional model of Kintsch and van Dijk (1978), who sees text comprehension only as linking propositions, the following two textual examples would have to be drawn from an experiment by Sanford and Garrod (Sanford & Garrod, 1981; Garrod, 1982) can be processed with exactly the same speed, since the propositional structure is the same in both cases:

- Anna was on her way to school. She was worried about the mathematics lesson. She was afraid she would not be able to control the class.
- The teacher was on her way to school. She was worried about the mathematics lesson. She was afraid she would not be able to control the class.

Subjects need significantly more time to read the last sentence in Example 1 than in Example 2. In Example 1, the last sentence presents difficulties because the readers imagine Anna in the role of the student based on the first two statements. However, it does not belong to the role of a student to control a school class. Therefore, the last sentence can not merely be processed unhindered, because, based on the last information, a reinterpretation of what has been read so far must be made. In Example 2, on the other hand, this difficulty is not present since the last statement is congruent with the educated model of the teacher role, and no reinterpretation has to be made. Further research has shown that information that is inconsistent in time, space, and also emotionally inconsistent leads to longer processing times. They thus refuted a purely sequential-proportional model of language understanding.

However, the appropriateness of an exclusively additive model of textual understanding is doubtful for other reasons. Thus, in the propositional model of Kintsch and van Dijk (1978), it is assumed that statements read so far are always mentally present to the same extent.

However, it has been shown (Lesgold, Roth, & Curtis, 1979) that in a thematically continuous presentation, relatively much information from previous sentences remains present, while this mental presence in a change of subject or a change in the context no longer given us. Depending on the content and context of a statement, propositional structures are processed differently and remain present in the working memory for different periods.

Overall, it can, therefore, be said that understanding has to involve more than simply linking propositions. Even though propositional representations have an empirically demonstrable significance for the understanding of linguistic manifestations, understanding goes beyond this:

Humans start from the very first information they receive, ideas about what might be meant; they go far beyond what is explicitly said or written. Implicitly, assumptions about the consistency and congruence of situations and contents are also automatically made, which lead to a delay of mental processing during topic changes, changes of context, and so on, and that not all verbal statements are equally present in working memory, All of these processes hinder a purely additive processing and understanding of individual propositions, as postulated by the additive model.

Because of these problems, various approaches have been developed to understand better and explain these phenomena. Common to these further approaches is that they all assume that the complexity and integrity of mental representations do not add up as in the propositional model, but are there from the beginning. As the preceding examples have shown, people from the very beginning make complex notions of a situation that may already apply to information that has already been obtained, and not put it together afterward.

# Understanding about mental models

Sanford and Garrod (1981) talk in this context of so-called 'scenarios', which are activated in the understanding. These are understood to mean holistic representations of complex issues, similar to 'frames' and 'scripts' (Minsky, 1975; Schank & Abelson, 1977).

If a suitable scenario is found for any information, the recipient of the information also tries to draw any further information to this scenario and thereby expand and specify the understanding. By activating such scenarios in the process of understanding, the mental representation of a situation goes beyond what is explicitly stated, as evidenced by numerous experimental findings (Garrod & Sanford, 1983).

Van Dijk and Kintsch (1983) have also extended their earlier propositional model, suggesting that propositional representation is complemented by so-called 'situational models' that represent holistic mental models of the situation. Understanding something similar to Collins et al. (Collins, Brown, & Larkin, 1980) under the term 'internal text model.' They point out that the internal model construction has a momentum of its own: As long as the information processing has not been completed, the internal text model under construction still contains spaces. Because of these gaps in knowledge, a person now has very specific expectations of further information, which is not simply passively awaited, but actively sought.

As understanding increases, more and more precise hypotheses about what is missing and expected to be information are being developed. Understanding is, therefore, not simply a receptive but essentially an act of the process, in which the receiver is just as involved as the sender of the information.

The conceptual differences between the different terms 'scenario', 'situation model,' and 'internal text model' are so small that I will follow SCHNOTZ (1988). And will only use the term 'menta-les model' by Johnson-Laird (1983) and which seems to be most appropriate for the characterization of this type of representation.

The statements made so far have not stated anything about how a linguistic utterance is represented in a mental model (En-gelkamp & Pechmannn, 1993). Johnson-Laird (1983) assumes that a mental model is fundamentally different in structure and function from propositional representation.

A propositional representation consists of discrete units of meaning, the propositions, which in turn are built up of linguistic symbols. The syntax determines how the individual units of meaning are put together, thus describing the intended facts of a verbal utterance. For this reason, the propositional representation has relatively proximity to the linguistic structure of the text defined by it.

A mental model, on the other hand, is an 'inner object' that, utilizing the analogy with the original (a behavioral, functional, or structural analogy), can solve tasks and problems vicariously and mentally in this inner object. The exact structure of the mental model is not important as long as there is an analogy between the model and the original.

The difference between the proposition and the mental model is well illustrated by the well-known analogy of feeling 'anger' or 'anger' with the concept 'heat,' which was underpinned by Kövecses and Lakoff (Lakoff, 1987).

Numerous linguistic expressions in English, as well as in German, indicate that feelings such as anger are cognitively structured as if they were hot liquids or heatable objects that must be handled with appropriate caution.

This shows u.a. on the following expressions: 'boiling with rage', 'heated debates', 'boil the blood', 'bursting with rage', etc .. Accordingly, you attack angry people, with glove,' and let them first you 'cool your little one' before continuing to talk. In the propositional model, it is now central, how exactly the linguistic-syntactic structure of the individual utterances looks like and how the linguistic symbols are related to each other.

The mental model, on the other hand, does not care about these structural aspects of representation as such the - in this case, functional - analogy of the original, that is, the emotion 'anger' or 'anger' and the model, that is, the properties of heat Objects, is preserved.

The two forms of representation thus differ, above all, in their quality. Whereas a mental model concretizes and contextualizes a linguistic utterance via the formation of analogy and thus always has certain imaginative content. A propositional representation is rather abstract in comparison, but much more precise in the depiction of the linguistic text structure.

Another important difference is that mental models, in contrast to propositional representations, allow not only the mapping of structures but also of processes. Thanks to the mental re-presentation, a process can be simulated before the 'mental eye.'

At the same time, the simulation of processes and actions can already make learning possible and may already lead to new mental models, a series of experimental investigations have been carried out (Brooks, 1968, Kosslyn, Ball, & Reiser, 1978, Metzler, 1973, Shephard & Cooper, 1982). It could be proved that in mental simulations of movements (for example, the execution of the movements in the high jump), the time required for a shift in mind is actually proportional to the corresponding physical movement.

In other words, mental stimulation, so to speak, takes place in 'real-time', although it 'only' runs off in the mind's eye, and is a testament to the fact that mental models are not only formed and psychologically real, but apparently also have close proximity to the original. From the various findings, it can be concluded that in mental simulation cognitive processes take place that is analogous in terms of requirements and course to actual movements.

## Mental models and problem solving

Due to the above, it should not come as a surprise that mental models can also have an effect on problem-solving behaviour and on the regulation of action. This aspect, which is central to the operational environment, is to be further elaborated here. Researches by Gentner and Gentner (1983), which asked test subjects how to explain the operation of a switch to switch an electric lamp on and off, show this connection between mental models and problem-solving.

It has been shown that many people imagine the circuit in the metaphor of the watercourse. In this analogy of circuit and watercourse, the cables are equated with tubes in which the water flows in a certain direction.

An electrical load then corresponds to a type of watermill that is put into operation because the water (the stream) is in motion. In this model, the power voltage corresponds to the water pressure that arises from a (power) source, such as a battery, which itself can be thought of as a kind of water tank.

Finally, in this metaphorical model, the switch is a type of valve that interrupts the flow of water as soon as the valve is closed. It would be conceivable and explainable why a consumer no longer functions when the circuit is interrupted with the switch: the (electric) flow stops and the consumer is no longer powered on.

An alternative to the metaphor of the watercourse model is the idea that electric current consists of a multitude of small 'males' that crowd through corridors (cables). The voltage would correspond here to the pressure to which the mass of males is exposed. Closed or open doors would act as switches, and constrictions in the corridors would function as electrical resistors.

Both analogies - watercourse and masculine imagery - are physically incorrect mappings of an electrical switch. Nevertheless, they are suitable as analogies to solve practical problems. Thus, in the event of lamp failure, despite the new light bulb, the heuristic would be suggested in both cases to check that the switch is closing the circuit. The fact that the physical processes are not correctly accounted for or understood is irrelevant for the elimination of the error and for the ability to act.

With these experiments, the importance of mental models becomes clear for human beings. Gentner (1983) have taken their research a step further. The test subjects should not only state what ideas of electricity they have but should also judge how the current changes concerning a comparison circuit in four different circuits.

The problem here was the differentiation of parallel and serial combinations: While the serial combinations of both mental models can be derived equally well (more batteries lead to more power, more resistors to less amperage), this does not apply to the parallel combinations.

Two parallel batteries produce the same amount of current as one, but two parallel resistors provide a higher current than a resistor. The effect of parallel batteries should, therefore, be easier to derive from the watercourse model, the effect of simple resistances, however, easier from the male model. The results of the experiment actually met the expectations: people with a watercourse model solved the battery tasks better, but persons with a male model solved the resistance tasks.

This experiment shows a central feature of mental models: The mental models not only allow finding suitable heuristics for problem-solving, but they also weight the different aspects of the same subject matter differently depending on the chosen mental model. This directs the user to specific solutions while others are out of focus. Moreover, as the examples above have shown, not every mental model is equally well suited to any problem-solving.

These investigations also shed light on how Misunstand can be explained on the level of mental models: Different mental models of the same subject inevitably lead to mismatches and are thus a potential source of misunderstandings. Besides, mental models not only produce a different situational view and a different evaluation of the context.

They also lead, as the above examples have shown, to a different orientation of attention. So if there is a misunderstanding between two people due to different mental models, then these people will most likely try with very different strategies to resolve the misunderstanding, as they suspect the problem in different places due to their mental models.

Mental models are thus capable of elucidating those processes of misunderstanding that are not caused by missing information or different terms, but by conceptual failures that lead to false implicit assumptions and inferring inferences.

# Metaphors: the linguistic representation of mental models

An important question remains unanswered: the question of how mental models are represented in terms of language and how correspondingly the processes of understanding or misunderstanding on the basis of different mental models can be grasped and analyzed based on linguistic utterances. The following explains why metaphors are suitable for the analysis of mental models. Using so-called knowledge management projects in companies illustrates how an analysis of metaphors can be used to show a different understanding of the same subject and to clarify any misunderstandings associated with it.

As the above examples of mental models of the electric circuit (Gentner & Gentner, 1983) have already made clear, metaphors are quite central linguistic instruments of analogy formation. Metaphors allow us to communicate and reflect on maternal models. They are thus one of the most important linguistic instruments of knowledge representation and central to every form of learning and every process of knowledge exchange.

In cognitive linguistics and cognitive psychology, metaphors are understood as analogies in which a so-called region of origin (for example, the water cycle) is mapped onto a target area (for example, the circuit). In this transfer process, the cognitive typology of the structural film of the region of origin is projected with its 'slots' onto a target area. This process of metaphor formation via analogies can be explained again using the example of the metaphor model 'money is water.' In this metaphor model, 'water' is the area of origin and 'money' the target area.

The three slots of the area of origin are thus transferred to the target area, and the abstract good 'money' is cognitively structured and understood in analogy to the watercourse. As the above example shows, not every slot of the originating area must necessarily be occupied in the target area. So there is no metaphor 'money sea' in German. Due to the underlying metaphorical model of money = water, the term 'money sea' would nevertheless be understood. Conversely, however, in the metaphorical transmission process in the target area, no new slots can be formed that are not already given by the area of origin, because otherwise the underlying analogy of origin and destination would be omitted. The metaphorical expressions thus formed would be incomprehensible. The metaphorical model 'money is water' has led to the formation of a whole series of metaphorical expressions in German, as the following examples show:

The source of money, the flow of money, the flow of capital, the rain of money, money can bubble, dry up, percolate, flow, be made liquid, someone can be liquid or liquid. With someone is low tide in the cash register, someone can swim in money; money can dry out or frozen, someone can turn the tap on, turn it off, and so on.

As the above examples show, these are the so-called lexicalized metaphors, that is to say, those metaphorical expressions that are fixed turns to the German language and are also learned as such in language acquisition. It does not include the metaphors that have been deliberately formed, as found in literary texts, or as they are often used in advertising and politics.

The understanding of metaphors presented here goes back to the metaphor theory of cognitive linguistics, as it was first formulated by Lakoff and Johnson in their 1980 publication Metaphors we live by. Their theoretical assumptions have led to a new understanding of metaphors and have inspired a wealth of publications and empirical research in cognitive linguistics and cognitive science, especially in Anglo-Saxon countries. The original theses of Lakoff and Johnson have been revised several times by the authors themselves and further specified (see Lakoff 1987, 1993; Johnson 1987, Ortony 1993). The approach of Lakoff and Johnson is based on the following central assumptions:

- In the formation of metaphors, originally sensual experiences (for example, the experience of drinking water in which one can swim) are transferred to abstract content according to the principle of analogy (for example, money, electricity circulation). Through this, the metaphorical transmission conveys a quality of experience as well as a help for cognitive structuring, which makes abstract circumstances tangible and understandable. Metaphors thus enable both complexity reductions and the creation of a meaningful reference to already existing experiences.

- The model concepts underlying the metaphor are not an expression of language but an expression of thought. They, therefore, refer to the cognitive structuring of experience, which in turn, determines action and thinking.

- Metaphorical expressions can not be arbitrarily generated and combined. What is considered to be an understandable metaphor and socially acceptable in a particular linguistic space is determined by cultural and social conventions, which are reflected in the lexicalized metaphor of the language and are themselves subject to historical developments. For example, the development of the car or the computer as everyday utensils new metaphors arose as gas, optimize interfaces in the team, and so on.

Further explanations of the concept of metaphors and the theoretical foundations of metaphors can be found in Moser.

Lexicalized metaphors have several properties that are of interest for the study of understanding and misunderstanding:

- The use of lexicalized metaphors is compulsory in both every day and specialist jargon. It is difficult to form a whole sentence without lexicalized metaphorical expressions. Thus, access to mental models through a metaphor analysis is possible on the basis of almost any linguistic material, irrespective of whether this is in oral, written, or electronic form.

- Metaphors and their correct use are learned implicitly through imitation in language acquisition and later further differentiated and expanded based on experience, for example, in the context of professional socialization and the acquisition of a specific subject-specific language. In this way, specific cultural and subculture-specific peculiarities emerge in the specific metaphor used of a person, which has emerged from a specific context of experience and action.

- The use of lexicalized metaphors is usually unconscious and automated, as is the application of grammar and syntax rules. The mental models underlying the metaphor and their significance for the understanding of complex and abstract facts usually become conscious only when learning a foreign language or due to special pieces of training (such as the metaphors workshop presented below). Thus, the use of metaphors should hardly or only to a limited extent, be subject to self-presentation strategies. Should, therefore, allow a relatively 'unadulterated' access to the implicit knowledge represented in the mental models.

Despite these important properties of metaphors, and although there are too many theoretical approaches to countless approaches, especially in cognitive psychology, cognitive metaphor theory has so far been perceived only marginally in psychology. Theoretical references are in psychology, as already shown, in particular to the theory of mental models, to work on analog closure and problem-solving and the schema term in cognitive psychology (Anderson, 1996). An overview of psychological work on the meaning and effect of metaphors can be found in Moser (Moser, 2001b).

## The function of metaphors for knowledge representation

Under the current buzzword 'knowledge management' projects in many companies and organizations are about making the knowledge of people involved in the work process more visible; thus better sharing knowledge, documenting existing knowledge and generating new knowledge in the work process (Moser, 2002, Moser, Clases, & Wehner, 2000). The knowledge of the employees and especially the implicit knowledge and experience are among the most important resources of a company and are central to long-term success (Moser, 2001a, 2003, in press). Ultimately, knowledge management companies hope for economic gain when, through improved knowledge sharing and better exploration of existing knowledge, knowledge loss can be minimized, and fateful and costly misunderstandings prevented. Since many companies are increasingly working in interdisciplinary teams and the individual team members often have to work in different locations and primarily have to communicate electronically, the communication skills of the individual employees are subject to ever-greater demands. One of the biggest challenges for successful knowledge management is the so-called implicit knowledge of the employees, as reflected in mental models, for example, because this knowledge is difficult to grasp (Moser, in preparation). Experts are characterized by the ability to efficiently and quickly arrive at the right problem solutions based on their mental models, which they have built up over many years of experience.

If this implicit knowledge contained in mental models is to be made explicit, the language is of crucial importance. On the one hand, language is the medium in which different implicit perspectives on the same object and implicit knowledge about this object are depicted. In knowledge management projects, implicit knowledge must, therefore, be captured to a significant extent via an analysis of the respective audio-specific language. Communication and language-analytical procedures are, therefore, central methods in knowledge management. On the other hand, language is also largely the medium of the representation of implicit knowledge as well as the medium of reflection and discussion of the meaning of this implicit knowledge.

It is outlined below how m e t a p h e rs can be used to analyze mental models and to explain implicit knowledge. The metaphor analysis has an advantage over other language-analytical methods that it can be supplemented and supported very well with pictorial representations.

Specific to knowledge representation, there are several other points to mention in connection with metaphors:

- The formation of metaphors is one of the most important cognitive strategies for the representation of complex and abstract issues in both subjects and everyday language. This is especially true for such abstract terms as experience and knowledge, which try to capture knowledge management projects. Precisely because these facts are so abstract, metaphors are a central means of making them tangible, as they reduce their complexity.

- The formation of analogies in general and of metaphors in the specific is central to the acquisition of new knowledge. The analogy allows us to structure and understand the new and the unknown along with the experience of the known. It is, therefore, indispensable to constantly build analogies in order to remain able to act and to decide even in uncertain and new situations. Familiar metaphorical thinking models are applied to new knowledge, and the metaphors generated in this way are used to structure the new knowledge base.

- Each metaphor model highlights certain possibilities and excludes others. So the metaphorical model 'money is water' defines what can be done with money (flowing, freezing and so on), where it comes from (it feeds on sources), and so on. In addition to this representation of declarative as well as process-dural knowledge about money, the metaphor model 'money is water' on a more general level also implies that money and cash flows are as natural as rain and snow and subject to corresponding natural laws. It can be assumed that metaphor models also have an effect on the direction of attention and can, therefore, potentially be effective in guiding the action.

In the context of knowledge management projects and the processes of knowledge exchange and cooperation; It is important that the use of metaphors can significantly increase the vividness of a problem or fact, and thus its communicability and transferability.

Finally, the emotional content of metaphors should not be neglected. As the following examples of metaphor models of knowledge management show, the respective emotional content that is conveyed is very different and has a central motivational as well as demotivation function.

# CHAPTER 5

# CRITICAL THINKING

# What Is Critical Thinking?

We can read that the man arrived at the Moon or that he never succeeded, observe the report of the results of a scientific experiment, or we can watch on television what we believe can be a mass demonstration.

We can believe in it or not do it, taking into account that what comes to us from the media, what we read, what they tell us... all this can be the product of an error or due to biased interests or opinions.

Today we have to be able to doubt everything, reflecting and evaluating what we perceive or what communicates to us. That is why we can ask ourselves about the ability to perform this screening. What is critical thinking and how to develop it?

# Critical Thinking: Defining the Concept

Critical thinking is the capacity manifested by the human being to analyze and evaluate the existing information regarding a subject or given, trying to clarify the veracity of said information and reach a justified idea about it, ignoring possible external biases.

We apply critical thinking to try to discern the reality of what they tell us and perceive from the analysis of the reasoning used to explain it. In a manner analogous to what Descartes proposed, it is about doubting the information, dogmas, and absolute axioms that surround us until we ourselves can give them truthfulness or otherwise ignore them. With this, we seek to have a justified idea of reality and not blindly accept what others tell us.

This type of thinking, linked to skepticism, helps the human being to create his own identity, appearing throughout development and being especially visible in adolescence and from it. It is not about bringing the opposite to the world, but about being able to elaborate on our point of view based on the verification and contrast of data. What is intended with critical thinking is to eliminate fallacies and biases that compromise the objectivity of the investigated data?

Critical thinking is closely related to other capabilities such as creativity, logic, or intuition, allowing us to develop new strategies and ways of seeing and perceiving things. Having a good capacity for critical thinking helps us avoid conformism and move forward as human beings, avoiding that there is only one way of seeing the world.

# Critical and non-desiderative thinking

Before, we have indicated that critical thinking helps us not to get carried away by the opinions of others and consider this something totally true and correct. However, we must not confuse critical thinking with acting on our impulses.

While being critical of what is taken for granted is a great help to improve ourselves and create new ways of seeing the world, that does not mean that we have to depend on what we create without further ado. This could lead us to think that what we want or think about something is the truth, which in turn can lead us to commit cognitive biases.

For example, a person with major depression may believe that his condition will never change and that everything he tries does not matter. This does not mean that this is the case, finding (either alone or with professional help) in your life positive things that will help you improve your condition.

Critical thinking in itself implies being able to set aside the different fallacies and biases to focus on seeking a truth that is as justified and reasonable as possible, seeking evidence and evidence that what is said or done is true. It is based on the search for objectivity, bypassing the subjective and manipulative elements that other people or even one can introduce in the analysis of information.

**What skills does having critical thinking imply?**

We have made a description of what is critical thinking. However, it is worth asking what exactly is necessary to have it? Having a critical thought means that the individual who has it has some degree of the following skills or traits.

## 1. Capacity for reflection

To be able to have a critical mindset, it is necessary to be able to reflect on things in abstract terms. That is, being able to associate the information that comes to us with its meaning at both a superficial and deep level. As well as the implications that such information has with respect to the rest of reality.

## 2. Flexibility

Critical thinking implies the ability to doubt that what we perceive or believe we perceive is true, accepting the possibility that there are alternatives other than the one or proposals. Thus, some mental flexibility is necessary that allows us to visualize that other perspectives than usual can be objective and produce the desired results.

## 3. Logic and bias detection

The ability to visualize the logic or lack of it in the things we analyze, as well as the possible failures and biases the affirmations and thoughts may have regarding them, is fundamental in this aspect. If we are not able to detect specific aspects of the argument that do not just correspond to reality or to those that lack explanation, it is not possible to make a founded criticism.

## 4. Theory of the mind

It is necessary to bear in mind that all the affirmations and opinions are elaborated by human beings, who present their opinions based on what they consider correct. Thus, knowledge may be biased even on purpose, if an objective is sought with its transmission.

## 5. Ability to doubt things

In order not to accept any explanation, it is necessary to be able to question the truth of it. However, the doubts must be limited to the reasonable. Otherwise, the existing principle could be doubted. And while it would be a critical type of thinking, excessive skepticism would not lead to any resolution.

## 6. Motivation and curiosity

To doubt something, it is very useful that what we doubt is significant. We can be critical of something that does not matter to us, but the presence of high motivation and curiosity regarding the subject or the arguments given implies that we will try to find a truthful and justifiable solution.

# Methods to Enhance Critical Thinking

Critical thinking is a very useful capacity and nowadays very sought after by society, both at work level and in other aspects of life. Therefore it is of great interest to be able to enhance it. For this purpose, we have various activities and habits that can be useful to us.

## 1. Try to keep an open mind

We all have our opinions about our surroundings. However, to think critically, it is necessary to keep in mind that ours or the explanation that society offers may not be the only one of the most accurate. It is more complicated than it seems, but we must allow in our mind the acceptance of other positions, however different they may be from our own.

## 2. Try to train empathy

Being able to put oneself in the place of others makes it easy to understand how they have reached the conclusions they have reached. Some activity that can facilitate empathy is the realization of role-playings, theatre, or the expression and communication of emotions and thoughts to others.

### 3. Actively participate in debates

The best way to increase competition incapacity is to exercise it. Therefore, participation in forums and debates is very useful, when confronted in them the opinions, beliefs and data found by different people.

### 4. Analyze texts and videos

The analysis of different materials can help improve critical thinking ability. It is especially important to observe the possible objectives or the reasons that a person may have to create such material. You can start with simple material and clearly based on subjective elements, such as opinion columns or advertising elements. Later we can move forward incorporating more technical and apparently objective material.

### 5. Avoid bandwagon and underdog effects

Many people join an opinion because it is either supported by the majority or ignored by it. It is necessary that our thinking is not influenced by the fact that others pay more or less attention to the fact or information in question.

### 6. Question stereotypes

Society constantly generates stereotypes regarding a large number of issues. Try to choose one of them and look for information that puts it in question to see how well it serves to explain reality.

## 7. Search and compare contradictory elements

It is easy to find publications on controversial topics on which there is no clear or certain general opinion. Looking for two conflicting opinions and analyzing each one of them allows us to observe what weaknesses these arguments have, helping to be able to analyze other future information.

## 8. Research and train

In order to discuss something, it is necessary to know what we are talking about. Being informed about what is happening in the world will allow us to put into perspective the information we receive from abroad, including the medium through which we have been informed.

## 9. Learn to separate information from what it causes you

Emotions help us give an internal meaning to what happens to us, and we live. However, in many cases, they cause us to behave or think in a certain way solely based on these feelings. This can lead us to consider what something makes us feel like the only truth.

## 10. Try to listen to your intuition

Despite what has been said in the inner point, sometimes our mind acts in a concrete way that we cannot explain rationally. Intuition is sometimes conceptualized as the result of the unconscious processing of information, that is, as the realization of an internal analysis of information that we have not processed on a conscious level. However, keep in mind that this intuition may also be biased.

# Ancient Mental Modes

Making a decision is as much art as science. The goal is not to make the perfect decision, but to learn to make better than average choices. For that, we need either luck or better mental models. And since having more luck is not on the agenda, we'd better look for ways to get better models.

It is better to be about right than completely wrong. (John Maynard Keynes)

The idea, in the words of Charlie Munger (billionaire, Warren Buffet's principal associate, and one of the most important contemporary thinkers), is to construct a canvas of mental models. His system is a sort of decathlon for the mind: not just a few areas introduced in school, but a broad range of fundamental knowledge about the world that will serve us in every aspect of our lives.

**Why mental models?**

Mental models are a way of analyzing the world. A set of tools to help us think. These models are not there to tell us what to think, but how to think.

All models are fake. Some are useful. **(George Box)**

The idea is to focus on models that can be applied daily rather than endlessly debating their accuracy. As historian Yuval Noah Harari explains, "Scientists usually assume that no theory is 100% correct. Therefore, the truth is a poor test of knowledge. The real test is its usefulness."

Even Einstein's theories were not perfect: general relativity explains how the universe works in most cases but is no longer applicable inside black holes in particular. But it remains incredibly useful, not just to improve our understanding of the world. Our GPS, for example, must take into account the effects of relativity to give us the right direction.

These models must above all be useful to us. Then you have to have several available. The nature of human psychology is such that if you only use one or two models, you will distort the reality so that it conforms to your model. At least that's what you'll think.

If the only tool you have is a hammer, you will tend to see any problem as a nail. **(Abraham Maslow)**

If your model directory is limited, you limit your chances of finding a solution. Paradoxically, the more you are expert in a field, the more this problem will be pronounced. Indeed, the more you master a model, the more likely you will use it to solve the problems you will face. Competent people in a specific area can quickly develop a confirmation bias that will penalize them when making decisions.

You can only choose the best tool if your toolbox is complete. Hence the importance of having several models at your disposal.

# How to Choose Mental Models?

Here again, we can draw inspiration from Charlie Munger, who argues that the basis of your intellectual pyramid should be composed of great ideas from major academic disciplines. Roger Kaufman suggests the same thing, namely, to learn the fundamentals of the three oldest and unchanging bodies of knowledge:

1: Inorganic systems (13.5 billion years) We will deduce the mathematical and physical laws that govern the universe.

2: Organic methods (3.5 billion years of biology on Earth).

3: The history of humanity (20-30,000 years if we consider the cognitive revolution).

These are the great basic ideas of each fundamental discipline, things that should have been learned in the first lesson of each subject. These are the general principles that govern the world. The fundamental laws in physics. The most useful mathematical tools. Important concepts in psychology and biology. The basic principles of the economy and markets.

Starting from these ideas, we can begin to build our canvas of mental models. The problem is the lack of good ideas; we all have them. But we tend to love our good ideas too much and use them excessively, which makes them as dangerous as bad ideas. Do not try to screw a screw with a hammer. Your problems will become much easier to solve if you use the right tools.

The famous investor and professor Benjamin Graham explain it this way, "You can have many more problems with a good idea than with a bad one because you forget that the good idea has limits."

The solution to this problem is to increase our repertoire of ideas and models and to put them in competition with each other. When you are in a situation where Model A will tell you one thing, and Model B will tell you another, you will be on the right track.

It is on these basic principles that we must focus your efforts. Behind every new idea presented as the revolution of the moment, there is certainly a more important, more fundamental idea that already exists. The "new idea" is just an application of one of the basic principles, packaged in a new sexier format. And yet we spend most of our time running behind the latest fashion ideas. This is true in all areas, whether in finance, health, or marketing.

It's not about suppressing our intuition or preventing our brain from operating the autopilot (we need it to function properly on a daily basis), but to use these models for important decisions. This approach of mental models puts things in the right order. Learn the basics first, then use this database for everyday decisions.

Here is a list of the most useful mental models.

General concepts (7)

- Inversion
- Second-order effects
- Circle of competence
- Ockham's shaver
- Hanlon shaver
- The map is not the territory
- Mr. Market

Mathematics (8)

- Compounding interests
- Law of Big Numbers (error of the casino player)
- Bayesian Inference
- Back to the average
- Game theory
- Normal distribution
- Thick-tailed distribution (Extremistan)
- Multiplication by 0

Systems (8)

- Scale effect
- Law of diminishing returns
- Pareto Principle
- Feedback loop & homeostasis
- Gresham's Law
- Black Swan & Antifragility
- Via negativa
- Lindy effect

Biology (3)

- The hypothesis of the Red Queen
- Number of Dunbar
- The founder effect

Psychology & Judgment (17)

- The Zeigarnik effect
- Fundamental attribution error
- The do something syndrome or naive interventionism
- Confirmation bias
- Group Thinking
- Endowment effect and loss aversion
- Pavlovian packaging
- The tendency to envy/jealousy
- Halo effect
- Availability heuristic (anchor bias and sunk costs)
- Forgetting the basic frequency
- Social proof (security in number)
- Consistency bias
- Retrospective bias
- Influence of authority
- Survivor bias
- Bias of excessive trust

Microeconomics & Strategy (3)

- Opportunity cost
- Comparative advantage
- The dilemma of the prisoner

# Learning From Critical Thinkers

Until recently, I had never stopped to question myself about the difference between critical thinking, critical thinking, and critical judgment. As stupid as it may seem, I have always made the duty to develop the "mind-thought-judgment" critic (s) of my students, and that of my own daughters ... without, however, know the fundamental differences between the three concepts. So I widened the subject, and I share my thoughts around the place of the school, including.

# The critical mind that nurtures critical thinking

At first, the critical mind is a general predisposition that the human has to interpret various realities, tangible or not, is a critical way, that is to say in a way to appreciate something based on criteria. Predetermined by the thinker. In this respect, the mind nourishes thought.

**Critical thinking: mobilizing reason in a reflective activity**

For its part, critical thinking is the capacity to mobilize reason in a reflexive activity. Indeed, in a world in constant turmoil, where we are constantly bombarded with information, it allows us to take the time to analyze objectively (or rather aiming at objectivity) what the universe sends us. It makes it possible to go beyond the simple theoretical and informative activity at the base of our own knowledge, created from that of others and from what emerges from nature, to question it and to draw, in a way, our own conclusions. According to an investigative activity. The goal of this exercise is to take action: "coherent relativism encourages action as much as the reason" (Barrau, 2016: 82).

The activity is rigorous and coherent: "coherent relativism (...) is an additional requirement. It does not deny the importance of the truth or its effectiveness within a system, but it questions, beyond the legitimacy of this system "(Barrau, 2016: 80). This coherence is confirmed by a rigor that makes the critical thinker go further in his intellectual activity: he verifies the sources, compares them with other sources, he identifies the nuances, he identifies the bases of consensus and objectification.

In the process, he becomes aware of his own biases and challenges them openly. He also crosses the opinions of others, especially at a time when so-called "social" traditional media are increasingly pouring into pre-formatted information in the form of editorials.

Critical thinking is, therefore, a complex intellectual activity since it is self-regulating, self-correcting, and resulting from a metacognitive activity. On the one hand, it allows a specific rectification of one's own thought to flesh out the quality of the conceptions of reality that are, in fact, dynamic. We correct our conceptions on a regular basis, and, beyond the awareness of our own cognitive biases, we use the reason to override them in our quest for certain truth, the most objective possible. On the other hand, this high-level thinking requires the ability to think oneself thinking (do you still follow me?) By adopting a critical stance not only about our beliefs but also about our own (meta) cognitive mechanisms. In short, critical thinking is the antidote to "magical" thinking.

**Critical judgment, or the search for objectivity**

Critical thinking leads to critical judgment, which is essentially a search for objectivity. This research is, in fact, a criterion-referenced evaluative activity:

What will produce a good judgment will be the use of criteria, i.e., points of reference or "reliable reasons," or in other words, the reasons for which the greater acceptance shared by Public opinion comes from a safe, objective and trusted character by subject matter experts. The criteria can be very varied in their forms, be formal or informal, but their primary function is to "provide a basis for comparison." To guarantee the value of judgment, they fulfill three conditions: adequacy to the problem, strength, and reliability.

**- Kerhom, 2016**

The search for truth is accomplished in the process of objectification in which there is a certain consensus in knowledge and sets various scales distinguishing what is acceptable or plausible in a given community from what is not. The objectivation criteria are therefore shared and recognized within the said community.

If we recap ...

The critical judgment, thus the culmination of the spirit that initiates critical thinking. When the mind triggers the critical thought and that it is translated into a thoughtful, objective, even perfect action (Aristotle speaks of entelechy), we go from the act which is essentially virtual to the action (what Aristotle calls "power"). The first act is the acquired skill. It's the potential and the ability to act, but without the action. It's the human potential of power. As for him, the second act is the competence in the action, the competence in exercise. It's human in power. The one is accomplished through his thoughtful actions.

From the mind to the thought, to the judgment that determines the action, the critical approach aims to make the human an improved version of itself, which, in a way, reminds me of the concept of the mentality of the growth of Carol Dweck (2006). Stating, essentially, that the human is a lifelong learner and that, thanks to this, combined with a reflexive thought, he is in continuous improvement throughout his life.

"Exercising critical judgment": a key competence of the QEP to ensure the sustainability of democracy

The critically-minded-judgment-judgment trio pioneered in our school thanks to the competence of "exercising critical judgment," the third cross-curricular competency resulting from the Québec Education Program (QEP).

If we rely on the ministerial document (2006), the development of critical thinking is essential because it is important "to go beyond stereotypes, prejudices, preconceived ideas and intuitive evidence to avoid that the mere expression of 'opinion is a place of judgment.' Indeed, we cannot say that our students are not critical. Criticism is easy: young and old have all understood this. However, to sit this criticism on an approach that aims towards the goal and from which one tries, by all means, to extract the emotional and the irrational, is another story. Clearly, it is easy to claim to be "critical" or claim to be critical!

High school students are at a time of development where they are particularly keen to assert themselves, to debate their convictions, and to have their legitimacy recognized. They are increasingly able to grasp the complexity of certain issues, to rely on facts, to focus on their own point of view, and to separate the emotional and the rational.

**Ministry Of Education, 2006**

It would be illusory to claim that one of the aims of the school is to develop critical thinking (as defined above at least), and it is for this reason that the school environment emphasizes the development of judgment. Critical, a manifestation of the early development of such thought. Studies must sharpen critical thinking.

Cross-curricular competencies, at least in Quebec, are the PSEQ's dislikes. However, at the time of the alternative facts and fake news, "exercising critical judgment" emerges as a key competence to ensure the durability of democracy:

"The true critical spirit, the one that helps us to thwart the alienation sometimes represented by the suggestions of our intuition, can only be acquired through persevering exercises. This work, so necessary for the advent of a democracy of knowledge, can only be done by insisting on it throughout the educational period and in all subjects as soon as possible. "

**BRONNER, 2013, P. 226**

## The role of teachers

Developing critical thinking in young adolescents, the same ones who learn to challenge the established order is a dangerous adventure! It is difficult to teach young people to develop this spirit when, in many cases, school strategy is based on coercion and dogma. We expect our young people to be docile and to respect the rules of life without complaining. It is also expected that they will assimilate all the content transmitted to them without questioning them. In short, we teach those dogmas, recipes, procedures without their having the right to question them. "Unfortunately, at present, and for ages, education serves a goal of social conformity primarily so that everyone remains in his place.

At the opposite of the spectrum, some, like Albert Jacquard, says bluntly: "the goal of teachers should be to make trouble." We must cultivate the doubt and teach why and how to question things to tend towards mental autonomy properly: "the doubt has heuristic virtues, it is true, but it can also lead, rather than autonomy cognitive nihilism.

Essentially, what is desired is that young people understand three things that are the foundations of critical thinking and epistemological reasoning:

- How do we know what we know?
- How is this knowledge validated?
- What does this knowledge serve?

Yes, "the critical path is narrow," but it is under the benevolent guidance of the teacher that the student will be able to venture there. The narrowness of the path is not necessarily related to the critical aspect of the trip, but rather to the scope of the inherent responsibility. "The aim of the school is, first of all, to promote the emancipation of a subject, a future citizen whose freedom and responsibility go together." In a society where there is much more emphasis on rights and freedom, the responsibility that flows from these same rights and responsibilities is overshadowed. Hence the importance, in my opinion, of developing not only the critical spirit but also the ethical spirit.

We all aspire, in education, for our young people to become responsible citizens, hardworking and productive workers, and open and empathic parents. These aims are noble:

The formation of the person as an independent subject who has developed the basic skills to be autonomous in today's world. And whose critical spirit has been trained by aiming at the acquisition of the basic knowledge to be able to learn all the life and participate in debates on the scientific and socially vibrant issues that cross it.

It has two important environments where this critical spirit can be developed: at home and at school. The school is the middle par excellence to achieve it since it is a social microcosm and an experimental social environment. The pupil has all the necessary supervision to learn and develop all these deeply human skills that are referred to when one approaches the question of soft-skills or savoir-être.

## How to develop critical thinking in class?

Critical thinking is a valued skill that does not develop on its own, of course. The teacher is thus invested with an important mission: to evolve the child's natural intellectual puerility:

But they [the students] will only learn to exercise critical judgment to the extent that the teachers themselves will be role models and given multiple opportunities to express their opinions, to discuss them with others, to confront them with different points of view and analyze their merits.

## MINISTRY OF EDUCATION, 2006

In class, students are often mobilized to learn how to solve problems. To do this, the teacher teaches them an approach that they reinvest in the learning activities imposed by teachers. These redundant activities, often called "drill" in jargon, are actually recipes that are taught and then applied. But to work on the development of critical thinking, another approach is needed:

It is better, for the formation of their scientific and critical spirit, to seek less often to put students in a situation of problem-solving, but in return to let them, at least sometimes, really carry out an investigation to solve them.

## CARIOU, 2004

Our young people, just like us, are exposed to the worst deception. And, of course, they are naive, gullible and vulnerable. They must therefore be immersed in authentic situations in which they can exercise their critical spirit: "To train the scientific and critical spirit of the students is good; to give them the opportunity to exercise it in society is better. One of the aims of any teacher should contribute to the student's mind so that he can naturally decide between dream, fantasy and reality. For example, teachers might ask them to analyze advertisements, infomercials, political speeches, public statements, debates, and so on. They could embody characters in a role play. They could design a marketing campaign for a multinational, or write an almanack or an astrology report. The possibilities are endless!

It is necessary to "teach young people the critical spirit, protect them against the lies of speech and print, create in them a spiritual ground where credulity cannot take root... and especially the warn against human testimony.

In short, the critical spirit serves the student to know how to protect himself against others, certainly, but also against himself, who might be tempted to miss his own "critical ethics." It reminds me strangely of the test of three Socrate sinks (assuming that it is indeed he who has developed this test!).

In short, what matters to us is to develop the intellectual rigor of our students, but also that they know how to take care of their word. We want to arm them with what is more powerful: a mind that knows how to doubt at the right moment, without sinking into mistrust. It is this same doubt that has managed to resist the worst dictatorships, and that ensure the preservation of democracy in our societies.

# Skills for Critical Thinkers

Thinking is something we all do naturally. The differences of our thoughts probably emanate from our prejudices and/or more or less erroneous conceptions.

Our prejudices and distorted visions could result from assumptions we made or from information given to us and taken for truth.

Questioning, questioning our assumptions, and the information we are exposed to will help us develop our ability to think critically.

Critical thinking is a very complex process used to understand better, acquire knowledge, and solve problems.

The process of critical thinking requires maintaining an open mind when collecting and interpreting data.

This process requires that each likely response be carefully evaluated to identify its 'likelihood of accuracy.'

Critical thinking has been defined in many ways. Some think that having a critical mind is a higher-order skill that makes it possible to evaluate the arguments and judgments that may lead to the formation of certain beliefs.

Others believe that critical thinking involves identifying and analyzing arguments using reasoning skills.

Both definitions imply that arguments must be examined to

determine whether the information meets universal intellectual norms. These global intellectual norms test the quality of information:

- Clarity of information
- Accuracy of information
- Relevance of information
- Depth of information
- Logic of information
- Importance of information
- Fairness of information

The concept of universal intellectual norms favors critical thinking.

Several other concepts emerged in an attempt to clarify the skills needed for critical thinking.

All involve an interpretation (categorization, clarification of meaning...), analysis (examination of ideas, identification of arguments...), evaluation (assessment of claims, evaluation of arguments), inference (questioning of evidence...), explanation, self-regulation (self-examination, self-correction) and deduction (reasoning by analogy, formulating hypotheses, modeling, forecasting...).

Although these concepts may explain the skills needed for critical thinking, the process of critical thinking can be more clearly explained.

Critical thinking starts with finding an answer to a question.

One of the most important techniques used in critical thinking is to ask questions. While the critical thinker might accept the first answer given, he will challenge all the answers given to him.

Critical thinkers must be able to maintain control of their mental activities, use their critical thinking to make sense of their world by carefully examining their thinking and the thinking of others in order to improve their understanding.

The critical thinker must be able to follow the inconsistencies in his reasoning.

# 10 characters you are a critical thinker

Critical thinkers are able to analyze problems from a variety of perspectives, resulting in more success in business and life. Discover your ability to think critically today. With these ten signs, you are a critical thinker.

## 1. You receive your messages from a variety of sources.

Critical thinkers know that partisan politics come into play in every mainstream media outlet, so they try to learn about the world from a variety of sources that offer different journalistic voices. They're looking for places like The Wall Street Journal for a Conservative Perspective, Salon for a Liberal Approach, First Look Media for a more aggressive approach to investigative journalism, and perhaps even follow the political thread on Reddit for a Smorgasbord that offers every conceivable taste.

## 2. You can have reasonable discussions with people you disagree with.

Critical thinkers are not afraid of a healthy debate. They believe any conceivable opinion should stand up to scrutiny, so they welcome talks with people on the other side of the spectrum. Although unlikely to change their minds because of these discussions, they are grateful for the opportunity to learn more about their fellow human thought processes.

**3. You are ready to change your mind if you find you were wrong.**

Critical thinkers know that it is impossible to always be right in everything. They are open to the possibility that no, they did not find out everything, and when that happens, they are ready to admit it.

**4. They resent people who resort to personal insults of commentary threads.**

Critical thinkers are often frustrated by the total lack of rationality that surrounds them on the Internet. While aiming to focus each conversation on the current issue, others inevitably resort to ad hominem attacks and personal attacks, and insulting tactic that makes a critical thinker slam the laptop and leave.

**5. You develop as a person every day.**

Critical thinkers wake up every day and are thrilled to have another opportunity to hone their thinking skills. They hide the shackles of their egos and wear an outfit of modesty because they know that they still have much to learn.

**6. You are fascinated by how things work.**

Critical thinkers have an insatiable thirst for knowledge. Her friends might accuse her of being bookworms, news junkies, or academic addicts; But they agree with that because they would not trade their childish curiosity for anything in the world.

**7. You have creative, innovative, original ideas.**

Critical thinkers would rather innovate than vomit. They value learning from the successes of others, but they make original ideas that are anything but "predictable" or "conventional."

While a critical thinker is typically a plus, there can always be too much good. These last three signs that you are a critical thinker are some common pitfalls to watch out for.

**8. Analyze problems that require only a simple solution.**

Critical thinkers are sometimes guilty of turning a small problem into a larger one. Your brain works at a high level, looking for complex solutions to the complex problems of life. However, the best solutions are often the simple ones.

**9. They expect too much of themselves.**

Critical thinkers are typically confident (and rightly), but sometimes they forget they're the same as everyone else (and just in case you were unaware, being human means we're all flawed by nature), We all have those moments when we lose our senses or make a bad decision; Being a critical thinker does not free you from this reality, but it often amplifies the following stress. Critical thinkers should cultivate an attitude of patience and let go of their need for perfection.

## 10. You do too much thinking and do not do enough.

Critical thinkers would be wise to develop behavioral habits to offset their tendency to rethink. No matter how powerful your brain is, it will not do you any good if you do not actively pursue your ambitions.

# How We Influence Our Thoughts

"He who can change his thoughts can change his destiny."

**Stephen Crane**

Our belief systems are socially constituted, and in this sense, we will be mediated or influenced by the specific historical moment, which we have had to live. What is posed from this perspective is that human beings are rational beings that can adequately process the information "we receive from the outside world," and which we access when we start our mental processes.

According to this, we can understand that our ideas or thoughts will then be nuanced by the information that we are acquiring from our socio-cultural environment, from what we observe or that we can experience through others, throughout our lives.

On some occasions, human beings start-up erroneous and distorted thinking processes, which lead us to invalid knowledge (in the form of dysfunctional negative automatic thoughts).

Automatic thoughts: they are conclusions, judgments, and interpretations that appear automatically when we face different situations. When these automatic thoughts are distorted, we tend to have adverse reactions, as if it were a continuum that generally affects our emotional state and on many occasions, our interaction with others.

According to Aaron Beck, these distortions of thought are described as follows:

## Hasty conclusions

To many of us, it has happened to us, that they introduce us to someone and for some reason, we don't like them, at that moment in our mind a message "sure you believe a lot" appears and when we know you more, we realize that we think wrongly.

Precisely this distortion of thought is present when we draw a contrary conclusion about a person or event without sufficient evidence to support it.

## Catastrophism

It has happened to you that you are late for work and the transport does not pass, or the traffic is hefty, and you automatically think "I will not be on time, surely my boss will realize, he will scold me, he will threaten to say goodbye and in the first chance it will.

As we can see, this distortion implies considering the worst possible outcome of an event (making a storm in a glass of water).

## The mental filter also called selective abstraction

Imagine you turn in a job at school, and the teacher congratulates you but makes some suggestions to improve your work further, at that moment you think "I don't know why I make so many mistakes if I had already made this observation" (omitting the praise entirely)

When we have this distortion, we focus attention only on SOME, mostly negative aspects.

**Magic thinking**

There are times when you are invited to a party, and you know that someone who does not as you will go, and you think, "I'm going to have a terrible time." At the end of the party, you get bored or angry with yourself, assuming you already knew what would happen, without analyzing that perhaps it was your behavior that did not help you to have a good time.

When you have this distortion, we believe that just thinking something and this will happen. It leads us to predict a negative result and believe that it is true.

**Dichotomous Thinking / All or Nothing**

Has it ever happened to you that you are preparing the food, and almost at the end, something does not go as expected (you forget some ingredient or something is spilled), and you think "everything goes wrong".

This distortion of thought implies the belief that everything is wrong or nothing is right, considering only one aspect of the whole situation.

## Mind reading

Imagine that you are walking down the street, and when you pass a group of people, you stumble, immediately you think, "They must think that I am a fool."

When you have this distortion, we draw an arbitrary conclusion that someone is thinking something negative about us without evidence about it.

## Overgeneralization

You have met someone who, having a bad experience in a relationship thinks "all men (or women) are equal" or "I will always be alone".

It is because this distortion leads us to draw conclusions based on little information and apply them to many situations.

## Disqualification of the positive

Imagine that you arrive at work and they are waiting for you with a surprise party, at that moment you think "sure they do it by commitment" (completely disqualifying the excellent intention of others).

This distortion leads us to reject or make less positive aspects or attributes.

## Magnification or minimization

It has happened to you that you decide to start a new

exercise routine, you arrive at the park, and after running a few laps you feel exhausted, and when observing other people with more energy, you think "I can't believe I get tired so fast, I don't serve for this".

This distortion implies the tendency to magnify our defects or minimize our virtues.

## Thoughts "Should"

It is widespread to hear that people always demand aspects of the personal lives of others, some people think "maybe they are right, they should already be married" or "they should have a bigger house".

This distortion refers to having internal expectations or demands about the behaviors or abilities of oneself or of others, considered as an unobjectionable code.

## Labeling

It happened to you to see someone lose weight and think, "sure you are sick." Or have you met someone who you suggest going to the psychologist and thinks, "of course not, I'm not crazy."

Precisely this distortion implies establishing negative labels for oneself or others, with which we describe their personality or behavior.

## Perfectionism

Have you ever met someone looking to get 10 in all their subjects to consider themselves a good student? Or someone who, when making a mistake, thinks "not to be good enough in what he does."

As we can see, this distortion implies setting goals or expectations that are too high on the performance of oneself or others.

## Personalization

Many of us have experienced a situation in which we feel guilty or take responsibility for something that does not concern us. For example, when we see that our partner is distant and we think "sure I said something that bothers him" (without considering that his emotional state may depend on something alien to us.

This distortion implies assuming causality in situations or actions of others without supporting evidence.

In the process of cognitive therapy, therapist and patient actively work to find these mistaken representations of reality so that with therapeutic techniques, the patient can improve their thoughts. Make them more valid or functional; in any case, it is sought that these thoughts are more adjusted to reality, improving their mental processes.

This process occurs as follows:

- The therapist and the patient collaborate to identify distorted cognitions, derived from assumptions or maladaptive beliefs.
- These cognitions and beliefs are subject to logical analysis and empirical testing of hypotheses (through experience), which leads individuals to adjust their thinking with reality.
- The goal is to correct the distorted processing of information, as well as the maladaptive beliefs and assumptions that maintain our behaviors and emotions.

# CHAPTER 6

# EMPATH

# Definition of Empathic

Empathic is an adjective that applies to an individual who manifests as the quality of empathy. This quality basically consists in the ability to put yourself in the place of another person, to try to evaluate the actions based on the situation that that particular person has around them. This type of quality is highly valued by the fact of building trust in the person who owns it; in fact, the empathetic individual takes the causes of others as his own. Empathy is also largely related to compassion, with the idea of sharing the passions of others.

Empathy is a characteristic that is usually present in some areas of art manifestly. Indeed, if we refer to the case of fiction, whether written or represented, we can verify that the best exponents in its generation have been characterized by the fact of being extremely empathic. In this way, empathy presupposes an in-depth knowledge of people. This knowledge, that leads us to examine deeply human nature, the fears, and hopes that move men in a recurring way throughout history. With this knowledge, a good storyteller can make your characters credible, act on mobile phones that are credible, and make readers or an audience feel reflected or represented in some way.

In acting, empathy can also be a useful element. Indeed, an empathic actor is one who can understand the emotions that go through people, emotions that must be represented for a certain audience. It is known that one of the main techniques used to develop a credible performance is to try to put yourself in place of the character in question. In this sense, the behavior before a fictitious personality would be the same that should be adopted before a real one; However, this process can only be effective if there is ample empathic capacity concerning people in general.

Beyond these concrete utilities, the truth is that empathy is a basic condition of any morality. Indeed, every position that can serve the common good is based on the fact that the conditions to which all men are subjected are similar in a profound sense, a circumstance that an empathic individual recognizes profoundly.

# Application Of Empathy In Different Areas Of Life

**In psychotherapy** means empathy strategy mood transferring the patient to the doctor. This allows the therapist to experience the emotions and mood of patients and, therefore, to understand they better. It is an active process of empathic understanding. This is necessary because patients deny that stressful emotions usually refuse to fight or avoid. The therapist must, therefore, adopt a correction, accepting, and appreciative attitude so that he can better understand stressful emotions and more effective appropriate therapeutic measures.

**In management** and in particular, in the direct management of staff who play motivation, involvement, and motivation of employees play a central role. The motives and motives of the employees on which their behavior is based cannot be directly observed; they can be tapped only through empathy considerably. Also, many designs are affected and may vary depending on the situation. In principle, other people can only attract (or prevent demotivation), if it is understood not only rationally, but also Imitation. For these reasons, empathy is an essential part of leadership.

**In marketing**, especially in personal sales and marketing knowledge and technology-intensive products and services, the employees in question must empathize very well with the thoughts and feelings of the customer and the offer to possibly adjust to the - often unspoken - to adjust to motives and wishes. Empathy is, therefore, an essential condition for the

Efficient organization of the sales process and particularly important in the development of sales skills.

As an example from psychology, the concept of "or social intelligence", the premise of the research on "Emotional Intelligence" by David Wechsler, argued that an important role, both in this discipline and in management theory, assumes and today the day under the keywords "self-regulation" and "Volition" have changed.

# The Importance Of Empathy And How To Develop It

Many define themselves as empathic, but few are willing to understand each other in a couple or family quarrel. Some people understand each other only when one has experienced a similar situation. On the other hand, empathy is practiced and developed. It is not necessary to experience a similar situation to understand what the other feels.

Empathy is important for a healthy relationship, lasting friendship, and harmonious working relationships.

Each is forging a reality of its own. Our genes and our environment define us. We are influenced by the environment more than we think. For example, culture, people we meet, marketing, the economic context, our education have an impact on our way of seeing the world. Moreover, many of the prejudices one may have about others are, in fact, a social construct.

Empathy helps to understand the other person and to see through his eyes his perception of the world. According to the Larousse, empathy is: "[the] intuitive faculty to put oneself in the place of others, to perceive what they feel."

Empathy is not to be confused with sympathy. Being nice is

feeling what others are experiencing, but you have to understand that when you feel it is with your perceptions. In other words, even if you live the same emotions of the other, you do not try to understand what the other lives in his shoes. We then tend to rationalize what the other lives, whereas to have empathy is often to listen and say, "I do not really know what to say, I'm grateful that you told me this».

Take another example: you make a road trip in the snow, and you do not have a shovel with you. A car slows down, and the driver tells you, "Oh, you're bogged down" and leaves. It is an act of sympathy. While another car stops and the driver gets out of his car to lend you a shovel. That's empathy.

Empathy is crucial because it helps us understand what others are feeling and respond appropriately to the situation. Here are 12 tips for developing it:

## 1. Be an Active Listener

Most people speak twice as much as they do not listen. Carried away by their enthusiasm, they leave little room for each other. And when they listen, it's more to answer than to understand.

While passive listening allows people to hear and respond to demand, active listening means that the person listens to each word, imagines the emotions that underlie what is being said, and retransmits regularly what is heard. Active listening encourages us to connect more deeply.

The more you listen actively, the more you will be able to read a person's emotions through words, tone, and expressions.

Becoming an active listener increases levels of empathy, but also helps to create positive feelings in the person who communicates with you.

**Six principles of active listening:**

- Forget anything that could distract you, devote yourself fully to the conversation;
- Maintain constant eye contact;
- Offer a real space of expression to your interlocutor by giving him the necessary time to express his thought without interrupting it;
- When finished, summarize what you understood and ask if it is correct;
- Ask relevant questions without judging;
- If the person is emotionally fragile, allow them to express and feel their emotions in a safe environment.

**2. Express Your Point of View**

After listening to the other person, you can express how you feel in the same situation. Imagine what your interlocutor is going through. Put yourself in his place, live the moment as if it happened to you, and let your emotions guide you. Once you feel these emotions, express them. The other person will feel understood and heard, and a true connection will be created (provided it is authentic).

## 3. Be Vulnerable

As we tend to equate vulnerability with weakness, it is an area in which we rarely engage in the risk of being rejected. Yet, it helps us connect to others. It presents us as human, with flaws, wounds, and fears. This feeling of similarity allows us to identify ourselves.

After listening to someone, think of a similar situation in which you have already been. Remember your feelings at this time and share them. Do not hesitate to share your interior landscape, your emotions, your insecurity, your fears. It is an ideal ground for a relation of quality.

## 4. Do Not Make Assumptions

To assume is to express preconceived ideas that are not based on any deep understanding. In this way, you take a shortcut to solve a problem without considering a more global vision.

When you make assumptions, you suggest premature answers. Take the time to listen and understand. Give yourself a moment of reflection to avoid getting into hasty and inappropriate explanations.

## 5. Use Your Imagination

Creating a connection is essential. But you may not be able to identify with a lived experience. In this case, be creative. Imagine this situation and the emotions you might feel. This projection ability is fundamental to developing empathy.

The commitment required by reading works of fiction promotes empathy. When a person gets lost in a story, his attitude and intentions change to reflect that story. The reader has the feeling of entering a new world because of the empathy he feels for the characters. This approach requires creative work. It is therefore about developing your imagination.

## 6. Spend Time Helping Others

Studies show that volunteering makes you happy. Putting yourself at the service of others increases empathy, and empathy increases self-satisfaction. Creating social connections with those who are not part of our immediate social circle and working to improve the lives of others contributes to our well-being.

## 7. Practice Benevolent Meditation

We know that meditation is a good instrument for mental health, but meditating specifically on compassion helps us become more empathic people. Benevolent meditation is a form of meditation that asks you to focus your thoughts on the desire for well-being for others. It's also a great tool for managing depression, stress, and anxiety.

## 8. Cultivate Your Curiosity

Being curious can help you increase your level of empathy. It turns out that empathetic people are also curious about strangers. The more you encourage your own curiosity, the more you broaden your network of knowledge and gain a broader understanding.

Be curious about the people you meet. The more you learn about how others live and think, the more tools you have to exploit empathy.

## 9. Try Another Person's Life

Experiential empathy is the most difficult - and potentially the most rewarding - of all. It involves changes in your beliefs, priorities, and relationships, and allows you to make new friends while changing your point of view. It means gaining direct experience of another person's life.

Imagine, for example, having someone else's life for a day. Try to consider all aspects of this new life and the possible consequences of your thinking.

## 10. Forget The Judgments and Criticisms

Declaring that just going forward does not make you an emphatic person. You must feel pain and distress. For this, it is necessary to set aside one's own analysis grid and refrain from judging or criticizing it.

Try to better understand each other's point of view without

saying it's good or bad. In this way, you will be able to reach a deeper level of understanding.

## 11. Offer Your Help

It shows that you see what the other person is going through and want to make their life easier. Providing help is an excellent act of empathy because it shows that you are ready to take the time to devote yourself to another person.

Keep in mind that we tend to want to fix what is broken when the person in need often only needs to be heard and recognized at first. Problem-solving can come later when a trust relationship is established.

# You don't want to kill me, the story about empathy

Look me in the eye and tell me if I really should die. What do you feel knowing that you are going to kill me? I know you don't want to do it. Make this a story about empathy. In your hand, is rewriting this ending.

Look me in the eye and tell me if I really should die. You know you don't want to kill me. You could take advantage of your work as an executioner to write a story about the empathy you feel right now. When you read it in a few years, you will be surprised. I imagine you will know what empathy is, yes, surely you know it. Try to put yourself in my place and try to imagine what someone who is about to die can feel.

Come on, dig into yourself, think that I can be your brother, that you could be me. The answer, what justifies my death? You point me with the barrel of a shotgun that isn't even yours. You have been told to kill me and do not hesitate to do so. Or so it seems. But I do know that you doubt. You don't want to kill me; you don't want to end my life.

We may be different, but you know that this is not enough reason to execute me. My body will end up on the ground emanating a trail of blood, and you will go to dinner with your family. You will know that you have killed an innocent man, and you can still eat. But I know that inside, you will be suffering.

In your story about empathy, you can talk about Robert Vischer, do you know who he is? He was a German philosopher of the nineteenth century who first used the concept of empathy. Although the German word he used was translated as 'feeling inside.' Interesting, right?

## I have no choice

«I have no choice, but you do. You can let me run away, and nobody will know. I will go far with my family, beyond these borders. Tell me, what do you gain with my death? What do you gain by shooting me in the head? Nothing, you win nothing, you might think that you are a good soldier, but, who is going to kill me, after all, it's you».

I want to think that if you were ordered to throw yourself into hell, you would not obey the order. Try to imagine that your criteria can direct your actions. That there is a possibility, more or less remote, that you follow that opinion that you have reached for yourself.

Who is your superior? What did he tell you about me? What do you know about my life? I will give you some information about when you write your story about empathy. Do you know that I have a five-year-old daughter and a three-year-old son? They are beautiful. My daughter, Luisa, always climbs into my bed in the morning and wakes me up by grabbing my hair. He tells me that his dad sleeps a lot. My son, Marco, laughs a lot with his sister. And now, you're going to leave them without a father. I will not see them again.

Tell me, please, do you think they deserve this? A father, you don't know; a father who has been told to get out of the way by having his own ideas, his own political ideology. You are mine, maybe not politically, but in this, in the human. I see it in your eyes. You have been told not to speak so as not to make love, but your eyes cannot help communicating: they have not left you completely blind. Your tense face shows that you only obey to survive.

«Little soul of mine, tender and wandering, guest and companion of my body, you will descend to those pale, rigid, and bare places, where you will have to give up the games of yesteryear».

**-Emperor Adriano-**

**Behind the tree**

Why do we hide? Why do you put me behind a tree? Are you ashamed of what you are about to do? Do not hide my death. Do not hide your murder. You have been told to kill me; that is how the country works now. Do it where you can see us, I want you to see how you end my life. Let them see your face when shooting; let me look at them when my heart no longer beats. Do not hide what you will do. No, do not do it. Do not hide orders.

I know you listen to me. Of course, you listen to me. In your future story about empathy, I know you will leave writing that you were listening to us all. It is unavoidable. You become brave before your superiors, but you are scared to death. The only thing that comforts you is that the idea has not come from you.

You think you only obey one order that your responsibility in this action is minimal. I would like you to answer me and tell me if you are so annulled if you really believe that because it is not your idea, your responsibility disappears. If they ordered you to kill your son, would you do it? You would kill him, not those who ordered it.

When you write your story about empathy, make it clear that the one who pulls the trigger is you. And that you might not do it because nobody else will see it — just you and me. You have options. You are part of a system that has made you believe that people like me must die. But you don't believe it, don't you? I know that it is not. Surely you are a good father. Tonight kiss your children when you get home. Do what I cannot do.

**Without rancor**

The night is about to fall, and you have me leaning against the tree. The sun goes down, looking for the horizon. I could run away, but I know I would end my chances of survival. In the end, we end up accepting our destiny. The question is whether this was really my destiny. How many have you killed before me? Were they all poets?

Do you know? I don't blame you; I don't hold a grudge against you. Maybe in your place, I would do the same, or maybe not. Don't think I'm mad at you. Now I am not furious with anything. I just want peace. My children, my wife, my parents... I hope you are well. I will miss you. At least you could tell them that I remembered them before, say, leaving. I hope that one day you will write your story about empathy in which you can see what you might feel, but that you are not authorized to express.

I think the time has come. You are loading the shotgun, and you are pointing me. You still have time. I'm still alive. You don't want to kill me, you know it. Can you really sleep tonight knowing that you killed an innocent man? Can you look at your children feeling proud of what you have done? You know you don't want to kill me. You could already have done it; however, you haven't...

"When the pure forms sank under the cri cri of the daisies, I understood that they had killed me."

**-Federico García Lorca-**

# Instrumental empathy: the basis of psychological manipulation

Instrumental empathy is very present in narcissistic and psychopathic profiles. They are people who intuit our emotional realities but choose to put them in their favor for an end.

Instrumental empathy is that dimension that often characterizes the psychopath or narcissist. Because beyond what we can think, these profiles do identify and read our emotions. Now, once they do, they use that connection to manipulate us, to take us to their land and reach a goal without experiencing any resentment for it.

In social articulation, empathy is in the quadrant of the positive and the desirable. We forget, perhaps, that less shining and complex reverse that presents this dimension. Thus, it is common to tell ourselves that people capable of harming others, whether physically or psychologically, lack that ability to empathize with each other.

However, studies such as the one published in the journal Brain and carried out by doctors Harma Meffert and Valeria Gazzola, show us something that should be taken into account. The mirror system, that is, the ability to tune into the emotions of others thanks to mirror neurons is present even in psychopaths who have come to commit criminal acts.

However, this connection is brief, punctual and aimed at specific purposes. Therefore, they would not lack empathy; on the other hand, if there seems to be a real concern for those who suffer, since they rarely identify with the emotions of others. What they do seem to experience is the clear desire to instrumentalize the other.

"Whoever fights with monsters takes care of becoming a monster."

**-F. Nietzsche-**

Instrumental empathy: I feel your pain, but I don't care

Thanks to cognitive neuroscience, we have made many discoveries in the understanding of human behavior. One of them is to realize, for example, that the empathic process takes place in many areas of our brain. Different skills are required to make contact with the realities of others, to know what the other feels, what he may be thinking, and what we would feel instead.

Thus, experts in the field such as Dr. Frans de Waal, a well-known primatologist, points out that sometimes these processes can appear differently in each individual. That is, there are people (primates included) who understand the emotional reality of their peers and are motivated to do something to benefit that peer.

Instead, others identify those emotions and choose to do nothing about it. They don't feel that need, that motivated behavior. There is also a third way. It is that which erects instrumental empathy and defines an individual who, being aware of the emotions of others, uses them for an end. There is an action, and it is none other than manipulating and causing harm without charge of conscience or remorse.

# Characteristics
# of instrumental empathy

People with instrumental empathy are often as charming as Sibylline. They are because we come to think that whoever we have in front truly cares about us. We convince ourselves that the feeling is authentic and that the behaviors they carry out are noble.

However, these behaviors have an end. These types of traits are, as we say, very common in psychopathic personality and even in narcissists. They can also appear in interested and selfish people. Let's see, however, what are its characteristics:

It characterizes cognitive empathy. That is, they have an idea of what the other person feels by looking at their behavior, expression, tone of voice... They understand but do not deepen, they never show an emotional empathy, where they «feel» in their skin what the other experiences.

Christian Keysers, from the University of Groningen, points out that people with a psychopathic profile feel emotions. However, their empathy seems to have a kind of "switch." That is, it is a process that comes and goes. When it appears, it does so briefly and on time, and when it does, it looks for a goal. They take information from us to know vulnerabilities and to be able to use, manipulate us.

That can we do before someone who does not empathize

"emotionally" with us?

Instrumental empathy is not comparable to emotional empathy. There is no deep connection, they are not put on our skin, and there is no express desire to promote our well-being. Moreover, what they will generate in the short and long term is damage, a violation. Therefore the question that remains on our horizon is: what to do before those who do not connect emotionally with us?

A study carried out in 2011 and published in the Journal of Personality, and Social Psychology showed that individuals with a narcissistic profile were aware that others did not have a very positive image of them. They knew they generated distrust. However, this did not worry about them. Even more, it was no reason to promote any change in them.

Therefore, we are facing personality profiles where we not only identify an absence of authentic emotional connection. But also, they do not mind generating damage or worry about the negative attribution we have of their person. They are highly pathological figures where many other psychological disorders are often constellated. Therefore, they will rarely take the step to seek or accept professional help to generate changes.

Randall Salekin of the University of Alabama, an expert in psychopathic personality, is currently carrying out mental "remodeling" programs to work on these aspects. The purpose is very ambitious: to ensure that authentic emotional empathy is activated in this sector of the population.

For our part, if we intuit someone who applies instrumental empathy, the most appropriate thing will always be to establish an adequate distance — a personal security barrier.

# Listening without empathy: emotional disconnection

Listening without empathy hurts. However, it is also worrisome that those in front of us understand what we feel at the same time, but nevertheless, do nothing about it.

Listening without empathy is looking without seeing. That is to say yes, with the face while the mind is absent, disconnected, and emotionally removed from the one in front. Few skills are as essential to building strong and meaningful relationships as communication and empathic listening, were to know how to connect with the eyes, feelings, and will.

Only a few months ago, Yale University psychologist Paul Bloom, a specialist in cognitive sciences, went around the world following controversial comments about empathy. According to him, this dimension has a little positive. However, to understand what he meant by these words, it is necessary to deepen his message.

According to Professor Bloom, at times, behind this dimension hides an act of sibyl in falsehood. One can, for example, empathize with what the couple is explaining to him, but give him exactly the same. That is to say, we all, in some way, are able to fit ourselves in other people's shoes, but then act with total indifference.

Therefore, we could conclude with a total success that empathy does not help much if there is no proactive attitude, an authentic sensitization, and an active attitude towards those in front of us. Moreover, as Professor Bloom points out, sometimes there are people who carry out certain behaviors based on empathy, but do not do them to help others, but to feel good about themselves.

All this perhaps encourages us to refine a little more the idea we have of this characteristic. It is not enough just to be there, to feel, and to show that we understand each other's reality. It is necessary to manifest that feeling, that bonding actively.

«The most precious gift we can give to others is our presence. When our mindfulness embraces those we love, they bloom like flowers ».

### -Thich Nhat Hanh-

### Listening without empathy, a sadly common behavior

Listening without empathy is something more common than we might think at first. Moreover, sometimes we tend to ritualize our daily interactions so much that we do not perceive that lack of emotional connection, which, almost without knowing, we are directing to those in front of us.

A very characteristic example is those parents who respond almost automatically to their children when they explain something to them. Are those phrases as manidas as " yes that drawing is very beautiful" or "really? How interesting », while they are picked up from school or while they are busy with other things and the little ones try to explain what they have done during the day.

These dynamics do not mean that we love our children less at all. It means that sometimes we don't have time to be present and we just listen without empathy because life is busy, because our journeys make our minds everywhere (and nowhere at the same time).

Non-empathic responses that hinder the emotional connection

We have all had that same feeling. That where we are talking to someone who remains absent, who says yes with his head while his thoughts are light kilometers away. However, it is common that there are other types of situations where they give us a kind of answers, comments, or reflections that, far from helping, act as walls. As fences in the emotional connection.

They are the following:

- **Advisory response:** What you should do...
- **Emphatic personal response:** You are an exaggeration, but if that is nothing!
- **Corrective:** What you say is not so
- **Interrogative:** And now, why do you say/think/do that?
- **Excuse answer:** I know what worries you, but I can't

help you right now because...

As we see, with this type of response, we realize that sometimes it is better that they had not told us anything. Thus, another problem is often added to listening without empathy: issuing answers that break empathic understanding.

**Cultivate authentic empathy with an active attitude**

We can all (and surely will be) empathic people. Moreover, studies such as that carried out by Dr. Anthony David of the Institute of Psychiatry, of DeCrespigny Park, in London, show us that it is already possible to measure empathy and obtain our empathic coefficient.

If we did, we would undoubtedly realize that we all have this dimension, but something we usually fail in is one of its key dimensions: social ability. That is, we are empathic, but we do not use this competition effectively. This sometimes means that we limit ourselves to listening without empathy, that we understand the other, but respond inappropriately or that the other person does not feel that we understand them authentically. Therefore, we need to keep in mind the following keys.

**How to use empathy effectively**

Empathy requires time and knowing how to be present without haste and excuses.

The empathic attitude is worth first of all the look. We need to look at the other without judging, with closeness and affection.

Second, we must know how to respond. Criticism, judgments, or "I would have done in your place" do not help in these cases.

In turn, empathy needs, above all, to be proactive. Because who does see that he understands but does nothing, cheats, and fails. Because to make us believe that we are valuable, but neglecting ourselves later, leaves a mark and hurts.

To conclude, let's not assume that we are all experts in this area. We always have something to learn, to polish, to improve in everyday practice empathy. Let us, therefore, begin with ourselves to give the best to others and thus take care of our relationships as what they are: authentic treasures.

# People lacking empathy, disinterested by others

Some people are a light in our path and others who become darkness that hinders our walk. Similarly, some people would do for us to the unimaginable, and others who would not move a finger for our well-being. The truth is that each of us relates differently to each context. Consequently, some relationships enrich our path and others that not so much; the latter can occur with people lacking empathy.

Have you ever noticed that there are people who do not understand that you make mistakes? Have you been related to people who don't consider your thoughts and feelings? These are people who do not have empathy, people who are not interested in putting themselves in the place of the other.

Empathy is the ability to understand the vision of the reality of the other to perceive and be aware of their feelings. It happens that there are people who do not have this quality, so we will tell you what these people are, what disorders may be associated with them, and how to relate to them.

The less empathetic you are, the fewer friends you will have, putting yourself in the place of another helps you grow as a person as our relationships flourish.

**Things that do not do without empathy**

People disinterested in others, could not get to have certain attitudes, because they do not have the ability or interest to understand and perceive the feelings of the other. There are cases of selfless people who lack empathy, so here are some of the things they don't do:

- **Worry about you.** They don't pay attention to you, or because they are focused on themselves, or because they don't care what happens to you.
- **Sensitize.** Although you tell them what you think and feel, they show no interest in perceiving and understanding what is happening to you.
- **Trust.** By not perceiving what we think and feel, those without empathy do not feel safe to expect anything from us.
- **Believe in the feelings of others**. People disinterested in others doubt our emotions. Therefore, they are cold before them.
- **Have compassion.** They do not feel an impulse to relieve the pain or suffering of other beings.

If you have these characteristics in mind, it may be easier to see in your environment who are not empathic. Keep in mind that for all types of relationships, there are nuances, there are people who have little capacity for empathy or too much.

**Lacking empathy, selfish**

People lacking empathy do not put themselves in each other's shoes. Therefore, disregard the feelings and thoughts of others. One of the most outstanding characteristics of the selfless in others is selfishness.

Thus, those without empathy can be very selfish because they think about their own well-being and leave the needs of others aside. Then, take advantage of the situation to benefit. In this way, they take advantage of us.

Also, they take to limit the fact that relationships have to be reciprocal. Then they only give if they receive something in return. Thus, they do not give details selflessly. They relate in a utilitarian way, making manipulation a way of life.

Thus, those without empathy can be cold people , since we experience the unpleasant situations in which we feel little understood because they are looking only at their well-being. These are unfriendly people who do not connect with others.

**Disorders associated with those without empathy**

We can all be lacking empathy, sometimes. However, some people usually carry this feature by the flag. Some psychological disorders are closely related to the lack of empathy; we talk about them:

- **Narcissistic personality disorder.** People are self-centered, have extreme concern for them. And leave others aside. The lack of empathy in this personality disorder has to do with not seeing beyond themselves.

- **Psychopathy.** It is that people cannot adapt to social norms and find it difficult to connect with others, so it is understood that they lack empathy.
- **Borderline personality disorder.** The person usually has emotional instability, so it is difficult to maintain stable relationships. They have more difficulty understanding and predicting how others feel.

Now, when you make an effort to explain to these people the reason why their reactions hurt you, they usually do not understand it and even make you feel guilty by turning it around, insisting that it is you who has misbehaved. Be careful; the lack of empathy can cause a lot of pain in those who do.

**How to face those without empathy?**

Some people lacking empathy not only have a hard time understanding us, but they manipulate us to get what they want, we give you some ideas to deal with these people:

- Set limits You decide how far people can get with you, don't let them pass from there.
- Choose your friends well. If you feel that you do not see beyond your needs, do not choose it. It will cause you discomfort.
- Assertiveness applies. Communicate what you want to say in the best way. Thus, it will be clear what you feel. In this way, you will not confuse a

person without empathy with the difficulty of properly transmitting what you want to say.

- Stay away if you don't feel an emotional connection. If you do not perceive that a connection of your thoughts and feelings flows with those of the other, stay away, you may face a lack of empathy.

Now the extremes do not lead us anywhere. Sometimes we can be wrong and see only our interests; it does not mean that we are not empathic. The important thing is to know how to choose which people are nearby. And, in whom do we place our trust because we know who we can count on in difficult times.

People lacking empathy are true disinterested by others. So, they are not able to put themselves in our skin to understand what we feel and think. Besides, they do not see beyond their world, so they remain in their comfort zone.

Run away from people who turn your speech around to make you feel guilty. They just try to take you to their land to get what they want. So, they are controlling people, and cold, who neither truly express what they feel, nor will they understand the situation you are going through.

# Great Readers Are More Empathetic

Reading and empathy are related. Admit it, if good readers know something well, it is that few things are as intense as those connections we make with the characters in the books, suffering their tragedies, moving us with their achievements and feats. That ability to empathize with these stories is also a way to grow, to evolve in many ways.

Doris Lessing once said that nothing manages to stimulate our spiritual, social, and emotional development so much as fiction books. The brilliant writer and winner of the Nobel Prize for literature could not be more right with her words. In fact, in a study conducted by psychologists David Comer Kidd and Emmanuelle Castaño, of the New School for Social Research in New York, the same intuitive conclusion is reached.

"He who reads a lot and walks a lot sees a lot and knows a lot."

**-Miguel de Cervantes-**

Fiction books, above all other genres, force us to immerse ourselves in a wealth of exceptional psychological nuances. The plot of the story, the paths of a narrative capable of awakening emotions , fears, doubts and passions favours an endless number of internal processes, introspective dialogues and dynamics that come to show us something that we undoubtedly already intuited: reading and empathy go from hand.

**Literary fiction improves our social empathy**

Possibly, no one had so much mastery when creating characters like Charles Dickens. In its extensive bibliography, we find the most varied psychological archetypes, the most varied, dark, wonderful, and perfidious personality profiles that we can find in any society. About 989 characters came out of his pen, and all of them served for several generations of readers to learn much more about human character, boosting almost without realizing their social empathy.

This is what the Kidd and Chestnut psychologists have been able to demonstrate. In their article published in the Science magazine, they point out that reading and empathy are intimately related because they help us to reflect on the conventions, stereotypes, and prejudices. To immerse ourselves much more in the intimate micro-universe of each character, understanding, empathizing with him, and sometimes identifying ourselves with their thoughts, opinions, and experiences.

Much of that psychological awareness, acquired in the pages of all those books that we "devour" regularly, we transfer to the real world almost without realizing it. It is a piece of baggage of wisdom acquired in fiction literature that also helps us deal with the complexities of our environment in many different ways.

So, if there is something we all know is that people in real life are not as easy to understand as in books. In our day today, there is no external narrator or an omniscient voice that reveals what is in the depths of that companion we like, that friend who fails us, that tyrant boss who asks us to reach certain objectives, forgetting the conditions in which we work.

However, great readers have special solvency to know what is behind certain behaviors, empathize much more, understand, discriminate, are alert, and are more skilled when it comes to an understanding of the complexity of human psychology than the one who, by example, rarely open a book.

"The less you read, the more damage does what you read."

**-Miguel de Unamuno-**

**Reading and empathy, a precious socializing influence**

The professionals who have been dedicated to psychotherapy for several decades explain that people's problems have changed over the past 30 years, as have the clothes we wear or the technology we have. We are increasingly affected by issues of self-esteem and emotional conflicts that arise from an unpredictable, nonlinear, and yet very interconnected world. The feeling of loneliness, fallibility, and uncertainty is robbing us of the internal balance.

One proposal that many psychologists usually make when they work with their patients is that they read. Beyond the therapy to follow, the person is generally recommended to increase their reading hours. The socializing influence of books helps us not only to reflect and understand much more this world, sometimes so challenging. It allows us to be calm, makes better inferences, develops reflection, and empathize with those who surround us and, above all, with our own needs.

Reading and empathy are healing. Reading and empathy are liberating; they invite us to deepen the dilemmas of life, we learn to be more compassionate, to connect much more with people to understand them, to learn from them, and allow us to grow, evolve spiritually as Doris Lessing said at the time.

To conclude, remember the healing power that books can have. Especially fiction books. Bringing them, for example, to the little ones from an early age will provide them with great psychological and emotional tools so that they also have a much more apt, sensitive, and enriching social conscience.

For our part, let's not forget how valuable the great classics can be for us. There are times when we need to reflect again on various questions about humanity, and for that, nothing better than to visit Dostoevsky, Tolstoy, Dickens, Chekhov, Charlotte Bronte, Jane Austen, or Herman Melville.

# CHAPTER 7

# SELF ESTEEM

# Definition of Self- Esteem

Self- esteem is the generally positive assessment of oneself. For psychology, it is the emotional opinion that individuals have of themselves, and that exceeds rationalization and logic in their causes.

In other words, self-esteem is an evaluative feeling of our set of bodily, mental, and spiritual traits that form the personality. This feeling may change over time: after five or six years of age, a child begins to form the concept of how other people see it.

The maintenance of good self-esteem is essential in any psychotherapy, as it usually constitutes a recurring symptom in different behavioral problems. Therefore, some psychologists define self-esteem as the function of the organism that allows self-protection and personal development since weaknesses in self-esteem affect health, social relationships, and productivity.

The concept of self-esteem is very important in the field of psychopedagogy. This discipline considers self-esteem as the cause of constructive attitudes in individuals, and not its consequence. This means that if a student has good self-esteem, then they can achieve good academic results.

Self-esteem is also usually a value analyzed from self-help, with thousands of books that teach how to protect and encourage it. However, there are sectors of psychology that believe that self-help can be detrimental to the individual since it promotes a narcissistic profile that affects social relationships.

# What causes low self-esteem?

The thoughts you have about yourself seem absolute realities, but they are not only opinions. They are based on the experiences you have had in life and the messages that these experiences have provided so that you form an image of who you are. If you have had bad experiences, the assessment of yourself is likely to be negative. The crucial experiences that help forge these negative or positive beliefs about ourselves are possible (though not always) to occur at an early age.

What you have seen, felt, and what you have experienced during childhood and adolescence, in your family, school, or the community, in general, have a determining effect when it comes to valuing yourself in the future.

Examples of these experiences are presented below:

- Systematic punishment or abuse
- Failure to meet parents expectations
- Not meeting the expectations of the group of friends and colleagues
- Be the "scapegoat" of other people in times of tension or distress
- Belong to families or social groups characterized by lack of affection and disinterest
- Be treated as the black sheep of the family or school

# How to be realistic to improve our self-esteem?

Improving our self-esteem is one of the pillars of many interventions in therapy; one of the elements that are part of the base on which we build the rest of the intervention. This is because good self-esteem strengthens our immune-emotional system and sustains our resilience, arms, and legs with which we swim. Understood its importance, now the question is, How to improve our self-esteem?

Achieving it, as well as facing other psychological challenges, requires that we implement various tools/strategies. This is because the sinking of our self-esteem can have roots in different factors. One of the most important is the system of powers with which we work and the degree of influence we think we have on what happens to us.

"Low self-esteem is like driving through life with the handbrake on."

**-Maxwell Maltz-**

**What is causal attribution, and how can it harm our self-esteem?**

Generally, when there is a deficit of self-esteem, we consider that what happens to us is a consequence of our own internal factors and that we cannot change. That is, we attribute to ourselves the cause of that "misfortune." Let's give an example. What will a person with low self-esteem think when suffering a breakup? Most often, in these circumstances, it is that he or she believes that the relationship has ended his fault.

Thus, negative thoughts of the type "I am not good enough for him/her" will appear, "I do not deserve," "I am to blame for this having come to an end." The reality is that when a relationship partner ends, usually divided responsibility. This does not usually fall only on one of its members, although one or both feel it that way.

In this way, when there is a sentimental break, it is normal for "thoughts of self-criticism" to appear. Frequent to this type of thought can appear precisely the self-esteem, that if it is healthy, it will lighten weight and avoid sinking. That is, we will be more realistic with the causal attributions we make in this regard. And the same happens for the rest of our life. People tend to make stable and internal attributions about what happens to them.

But not only that, but they also tend to make external attributions of that good thing that happens to them. That is to say, they believe that when they are promoted at work, for example, it is because their boss is a good person, but not because of their merits at work level. What happens with this? That way, it is impossible for them to feel good about themselves when they are rewarded or reinforced.

«Until you value yourself, you will not value your time. Until you value your time, you won't do anything with it.

**-M. Scott Peck-**

**Learn to modify the causal attribution to improve our self-esteem**

Now, what can we do to change our causal attribution and thus improve our self-esteem? Let's start by moving away a bit to take perspective. So we can make a general assessment and adjusted to reality and not only focused on failures or problems. As happens when we compare our life with that of others in social networks, it will be of no use to us that this causal attribution becomes too optimistic because then the clash with reality will be worse.

Therefore, we must question to what extent we influence what happens to us (for better or worse) and what other factors have intervened to give a certain outcome. Thus, we have to learn to attribute the good that happens to us if it is due to something we have done. In this way, we will learn and improve our self-esteem.

In the same way, we have to see if the bad is attributable to causes related to ourselves or not, to stop blaming ourselves for events in which our influence has been minimal or zero. Also, if in the event we do have a good part of the responsibility, it will not help us to punish ourselves after having analyzed the fact and having learned. This will make it more complicated for us to repeat mistakes in the future and for our self-esteem to be damaged.

«When you recover or discover something that feeds your soul and brings you joy, take care of loving yourself enough and make it a space in your life.»

**-Jean Shinoda Bolen-**

Following this line, we can continue to evolve and improve. In this sense, being able to analyze ourselves realistically will help us to have a tighter view of our strengths and weaknesses. This will improve our self-esteem and facilitate our empowerment, as we will be able to choose better the objectives in which we invest our resources.

# Strategies to increase self-esteem

Self-esteem, and more specifically, its state and its influence, has become a crossroads for many. Some countless books and articles show us as a panacea. If you have it, everything will flow, they announce. If you don't count on her, everything will go wrong. The problem is that self-esteem is built mainly in the first years of life, and it cannot be passed twice. That is why many wonders: is there any way to increase self-esteem when it is not well-grounded?

The answer to that question is yes, of course. When someone has highly favorable conditions, it is easy for their self-love to take root from the first years of life. This will give you particular strength and more chances of finding well-being and happiness. But if this does not happen, it is also possible to repair roots that are not so strong.

Another question appears on the horizon: why increase self-esteem? Although it seems obvious, sometimes it is not so. Lack of self-love is the seed of many inconvenient states, the factor that increases your risk. It also usually results in a constant nonconformity that finds no relief. Make it realistic to set realistic goals and achieve them. In short, it can make life much more complicated. To avoid this, we will present three effective strategies.

" We all know that self-esteem comes from what you think of yourself, not what others think of you ."

**-Gloria Gaynor-**

## 1. Develop a reminder, a technique to increase your self-esteem

There is a large part of our behavior that we are not aware of, or at least not always aware of. Most of the time, we can't say precisely why we think how we think or feel how we feel. We simply experience it this way and not otherwise, but we ignore why. All that information is in the unconscious, or at least an important part.

The truth is that when there is no self-love, the mind operates in such a way that it overlooks many positive aspects of who we are. That is when a reminder becomes a valuable instrument to increase self-esteem.

It is simply about taking a written inventory of the best of us. What you like about yourself, what you achieved today, the obstacles you have overcome. Specify what your virtues, abilities, and skills are. Write down your good deeds. And, above all, check this list frequently. You will help your mind to function as an ally and not as an enemy.

## 2. Identify destructive approaches

When self-esteem is injured, we tend to see the world from a very dark perspective. In one way or another, we project our discomfort to our surroundings. In this way, we end up focusing more on the negative than on the positive of reality.

There are also unconstructive habits such as comparing ourselves with others, getting scared when we are about to achieve some important achievement, or being carried away by inertia because we have a hard time believing in our own dreams.

It is worth keeping an attitude of observation in front of ourselves. The goal is to detect all those lines of thought that lead us to feel bad. Most likely, we will see black things not because they are like that, but because we have created the habit of interpreting them that way. By observing and identifying this, little by little, we are freeing ourselves from these destructive customs.

## 3. The exercise of the five fingers

This is an exercise proposed by the psychologist José Ignacio Fernández. It can be very effective in increasing self-esteem. It includes a series of very simple actions to improve mood when there is decay.

The actions to be carried out are the following:

- Relaxation. The first is to inspire and expire deeply to achieve a state of greater relaxation.
- First mental image. It is advisable first to extend your hands and then join the index finger with the

thumb. In that position, remember some moments in life in which we have felt loved or protected. For example, a moment of helplessness where another was interested in taking care of us

- Second mental image. Now you have to put your thumb together with the middle finger. Then evoke some situations in which we have had success or achievement.
- Third mental image. Join the thumb with the ring finger. Then bring to mind some noble act that we have performed.
- Fourth and last mental image. Finally, the thumb and little finger come together. Then you must remember someone who is truly loved or loved.

This exercise is useful in those moments when there are many reproaches or a lack of confidence in ourselves. It is very effective both to find a balance at the moment and to increase long-term self-esteem. Remember that, regardless of the circumstances, we can always change and learn to be happier.

# Self-esteem and depression, how do they relate?

Self-esteem and depression have a significant bond. Thus, and although the origin of depression is clearly multifactorial, clinical studies reveal that low self-esteem maintained over time makes us much more vulnerable to this type of condition. Not accepting ourselves and lacking positive feelings towards one's own, leaving us without psychological resources.

We understand self-esteem as that set of feelings generated by self-concept. In this way, while self-concept encompasses all that set of ideas and beliefs that define the mental image of which we are self-esteem, outlines above all a basic emotional component for human well-being.

Low self-esteem makes us feel bad about ourselves, generates disconnection, dejection, and great vulnerability when developing various psychological disorders.

Knowing this, it cannot surprise us those psychologists and psychiatrists take this psychological dimension into account when it comes to an understanding of depressive spectrum disorders. However, in the Diagnostic and Statistical Manual of Mental Disorders (DSM-V), low self-esteem is not included as such among the criteria that a person must meet to be diagnosed with depression. However, dimensions such as the "feeling of worthlessness" do appear.

Researchers of personality psychology, meanwhile, have always shown great interest in the relationship between self-esteem and depression. For the latter, the question would be the following: is self-esteem a factor capable of promoting depression? Or is it depression itself that ends up undermining one's self-esteem? Let's see it below.

**Self-esteem and depression: two models to explain their relationship**

Many times we get up, shower, have breakfast, and go outside without knowing that we are naked. It doesn't matter how warm we go or the brand that our jeans or shirts have if every day we face the world with low self-esteem. Because through its thin slits and weak armor, everything comes in, abuse, fear, insecurity, negativism ...

It is clear, however, that depressions have, on average a rather diffuse and multifactorial origin, without forgetting those endogenous factors that we cannot always control. However, no one can ignore that every mind covered by this low self-esteem results in low effectiveness in dealing with and managing the simplest problems. Moreover, the glass of these glasses by which the person with weak self-esteem observes the world is usually, on average, quite dark.

However, the only way to demonstrate that link between self-esteem and depression is through scientific studies, and especially through longitudinal research. Thus, and only as a more recent example, the University of Basel published in this same year a very illustrative work on the subject that can give us some answers. Let's see them.

## The vulnerability model

According to the vulnerability model, there are people with a personality profile characterized by habitually low self-esteem. According to this point of view, this psychological pattern will negatively process life events. It will also lack basic skills, such as resilience.

- They are often promoters of reality to defend against, to distrust, and in which to always position themselves as a victim or secondary actor instead of conceiving themselves as protagonists of their own stories. Deserving of opportunities and promoters of positive changes with which to overcome negative events.
- Moreover, the authors of this work could see that in many cases, people with low self-esteem tried not to refute but to verify their negative self-concept by paying greater attention and relevance to the negative comments of the people in their environment.
- Self-esteem and depression are related to the vulnerability model to designate those people without resilience and low emotional solvency.

## The scar model

Let us now to the opposite view. According to the study, as mentioned above, something that could also be seen in the longitudinal study is that depression itself is often the one who shapes low self-esteem. All that legion of desperate, negative, and exhausting feelings that orbit the depressive mind are those that directly undermine self-esteem.

What do we stay with? With the vulnerability model or with the scar model that advocates depression as a cause of low self-esteem? The American Psychological Association (APA) is clear: weak self-esteem is another risk factor when developing various psychological disorders, including depression.

Moreover, in one of the publications of this institution, he warned that self-esteem and depression are so strongly correlated in cross-sectional studies, that it is a priority to develop adequate prevention strategies in the adolescent population. The number of diagnoses does not stop increasing in this sector. And what is worse, also the number of suicides.

The vulnerability model is, therefore, what we should all keep in mind. Somehow, it also fits with Beck's cognitive triad model on people at higher risk for depression. Namely, they are profiles with a negative view of the world, people who do not trust the future, and who also perceive themselves as beings worthless.

These kinds of attributions, of such limited and gloomy approaches, do not lead anywhere. And less to the expression of a meaningful, optimal, and hopeful life. Self-esteem and depression, therefore, maintain a bond of union that we cannot neglect. Let us, therefore, invest in that plot of our personal universe. Keep the garden of our self-esteem strong, bright, beautiful in all its aspects and corners.

# Improve your self-esteem with mindfulness

Defining self-esteem is not a simple task. We could say that it is the emotional part that derives from our self-concept, that is, the emotions that are born from how we look. These emotions, in turn, would generate thoughts, behaviors, and emotions that would tend to reinforce this self-concept. That is why improving our self-esteem is such an easy and difficult task at the same time.

On the other hand, mindfulness encompasses a set of proposals with a common objective: to recover full consciousness, mindfulness, or attentive and thoughtful presence, which consists of being present in the here and now, being observers of what happens to us without judging. It's about us experimenting, having openness to the experience with the least possible prejudices and filters.

When you are no longer able to change a situation, you have the challenge of changing your attitude towards it.

**The ladder of self-esteem**

We will attend to self-esteem as a principal element, especially sensitive to five processes. They would be the following:

- Self-knowledge. Knowing ourselves, with our defects and our virtues. The positive or negative is part of our way of understanding life, not to be confused with the socially accepted. We can hear what others think, but it is we who finally introduces each element into its drawer, forming our ethics and thus conditioning our self-concept and our self-esteem.

- Self Acceptance. Accept what we cannot change now or that it is better not to change because really trying would have a cost in resources that we cannot assume. In any case, far from the projection of the future, the present offers us the possibility to reconcile with the person we are now.

- Self-assessment. It is the ability that people have to value our virtues and abilities, both physically and intellectually. This step is one of the most important: some of us have a hard time separating those skills in which we are good from those in which we are not so much.

- Self-respect. Many people think that they do not deserve what they have or can have. Respecting us means giving way to an internal dialogue that does not destroy us, nurturing emotions of negative valence or initiating behaviors that harm us to punish or rebuke us.

- Self-improvement. Getting to know each other is the first step to improve ourselves. If we manage to perform the four previous stages, we can enjoy a good self-concept and healthy self-esteem.

**Improve self-esteem with mindfulness on how to do it?**

Once we know the five factors that influence, and much, in our self-esteem, we will see how we can work them through the meditative practice of mindfulness. It is about working them one by one, based on a plan and following an order

To improve self-esteem with mindfulness we will perform a series of exercises and guided meditations focused on each of the components of self-esteem that we have been detailing before.

Guided meditations are a good tool to work on improving self-esteem with mindfulness.

· **Self-knowledge**

The practice could be introduced as follows:

- We will adopt a comfortable, calm, and relaxed posture, having our mind in the here and now, moment by moment. We catch air and are observers of our breathing, becoming aware of how air enters our nose and widens our lungs from the abdomen. Finally, we expel the air.
- In the first place, we will try to focus on three defects, and then on three virtues. Once we are aware of our defects and virtues, we will observe them as part of us. Remember that they are necessary and make us unique and special; Thus,

we will observe them without judging them, without judging ourselves.

We gently open our eyes and move slowly.

Duration: 10-15 min.

Understanding who you are is much more important than pursuing what you should be. Because if you understand what you are, a process of spontaneous transformation begins, while if you try to become what you should be, there is no change: only the old will remain with a different appearance.

· **Self-acceptance**

The process of self-acceptance is, without a doubt, the most difficult step of personal improvement. Almost all people want to improve something of themselves by not being happy with any content of their being, either concerning their body, their personality, or about their way of acting.

As with self-knowledge, we are going to do a practice related to meditation, but now focusing on self-acceptance. Accepting the qualities we don't like is not easy, but it is necessary to improve our self-esteem.

We proceed again to adopt a comfortable and relaxed posture. We take a breath and focus on our breathing. We leave our external prejudices and assessments behind and limit ourselves to accepting them. We accept who we are with our positive and negative qualities, our strengths and weaknesses, our lights, and our shadows.

We focus our attention on those defects that we have previously identified and observe and accept them as part of us. Let us repeat the following sentence when we observe the defect, "I accept myself completely and deeply" or what is the same, "I love and respect myself completely and deeply."

As for the virtues, we catch air again and focus on one of them; we watch it, watch and let it go. We proceed to wake up from this state of meditative semi-incoscience and slowly open our eyes, move our hands, legs, and other parts of our body. As we see, improving self-esteem with mindfulness is possible from self-acceptance.

Duration: 10-15 min.

Wanting to be another person is wasting the person you are.

· **Self-assessment**

This phase is not a good time to be modest, but quite the opposite. Take a notebook and write down any aspect you are good at and value it as it deserves.

Now do not worry about trying to rank these aspects. Each one of us has different qualities, and we must be proud of them.

No one can make you feel inferior without your consent.

· **Self-respect**

The needs and desires are inherent to the fact of living and are part of any path to happiness. Let's try to respect ourselves, look for our skills, and try to keep a space for positive Valencia emotions in any circumstance.

Let's try not to blame ourselves for mistakes and not to calculate feelings of happiness as opposed to other people. If we believe that we are doing something right, there is nothing wrong with feeling happy about it.

If the grass looks greener on the other side ... Stop looking, stop, and compare, stop complaining, and start watering the grass you are standing on.

· **Self-improvement**

As the last point to improve self-esteem with mindfulness, after having seen the different grades, we reach self-improvement. If the person knows each other, he can always improve himself in his personal life.

It is important, as we have said, to know, accept, value, and respect us. Only in this way, we can overcome and improve our self-esteem, which will help us make appropriate decisions and solve solvency actions or our daily problems.

As we have seen, it is possible to improve self-esteem with mindfulness. To do this, we must know, accept, value, and respect ourselves too, later, overcome. It is important to follow the points just noted. It is impossible to be happy with ourselves and to overcome ourselves personally if we do not, consequently, follow the different steps.

# Personal integrity, a pillar of self-esteem

To have proper self-esteem, we should work certain aspects, such as personal integrity.

For Nathaniel Branden, a renowned psychotherapist, a doctorate in psychology and self-esteem specialist, the development and strengthening of this is based on six pillars. The last, but not least, is personal integrity. We will talk about him in this section.

According to this prestigious specialist, to have healthy self-esteem, at good levels that make us feel happy and satisfied with ourselves, it is essential to work the following points, in the same order they appear:

- Live the present consciously.
- Total acceptance of oneself.
- Accept that one is responsible for oneself that is, self-responsibility.
- Pay attention to yourself or what is the same practice self-affirmation.
- Have purposes in life.
- Respect personal integrity.

To improve self-concept, and indirectly self-esteem, it is necessary to be clear about personal integrity. So the first step we are going to take is to define it from a psychological perspective.

## What is personal integrity?

If we use the definition provided by Nathaniel Branden, we will say that it is " the integration of our ideals, convictions, norms, beliefs on the one hand and our conduct on the other side. When our behavior is congruent with our values, when our ideals and practice agree, we have integrity. "

So, based on it, we will say that personal integrity appears when we act in accordance with our value system. Thus, if we believe that in life, one must act in one way and act oppositely, the dissonance is likely to appear an unpleasant sensation that generates a conflict with self-concept.

Now, if we proceed according to our desires and values, with the principles, convictions, beliefs, ideas that are paramount for us, we will be protected against this disharmony. Our vision of I will be aligned with the elements listed: a union that will transmit peace to us.

Of course, it is for this union to occur; it is important to be clear about your principles, values, convictions, ideas, beliefs. We talk about yours really, not those who have instilled or try to impose. No matter what family, friends, co-workers, etc. tell you. It is an exercise in honesty with oneself, the product of sincere, internal dialogue.

## Why is personal integrity a pillar of self-esteem?

"Developing our self-esteem is to expand our ability to be happy."

**-Nathaniel Branden-**

Self-esteem marks the decisions we make, impacting our health and well-being. It will condition our life on all levels: work, social, playful, etc. Besides, it will spread in all these dimensions through a backbone: the attitude.

Hence, it is essential that we have a healthy level of self-esteem and, for this, in addition to working other personal facets, the work of personal integrity is essential, since, the more our way of living with our values coincides, more health You will enjoy our self-esteem.

As we conduct ourselves according to our convictions, our conscience will feel good. In this mental scenario, it will be easy for our mental state to become infected, and also to recognize ourselves in what we do, reinforcing our self-esteem.

For example, a person places his trust in you, he orders you to do a job, and you do it well, in the time you can, without continually postponing it and charging him a fair price. This, in addition to making you look good with the other person and feeling the satisfaction of a job well done, will make you feel happy with yourself because you have acted according to what you think needs to be done.

This will cause you to feel good, improve your self-esteem.

In this way, you will identify doing things this way with that well-being, creating a habit that will make you live with personal integrity. All while your self-esteem grows, since you accept yourself, you value yourself and love yourself. That is why it is very convenient to work personal integrity, taking care of one of the fundamental pillars of self-esteem.

# Relationship between low self-esteem and self-sabotage

The relationship between low self-esteem and self-sabotage forms a lethal alliance. To the insecurity are added those obsessive and persistent thoughts that dare to take away values, opportunities, and potential. It is like living under the perpetual domain of fear.

Low self-esteem and self-sabotage constitute a two-headed creature capable of devouring all human potential, all worth, and personal integrity. The lack of self-confidence and insecurity is often accompanied by a voiceover that, with a malevolent tone, tells us, almost every moment, that we are fallible, that we will achieve nothing, that it is useless to have hope and hope.

If we could put a speaker to the thoughts of at least 50% of the people we meet daily, we would discover something revealing and scary at the same time. In their minds, there would be no lack of limiting thoughts, negative self-assessments, and self-criticism. We all, somehow, act as enemies at some time during the day.

Self-sabotage is common, and as such, we can open the door to this uncomfortable tenant at some point in time. Now, the problem occurs when we grant excessive power and give that weak voice a fixed place in our lives. No one deserves an existence where you stand as your worst enemy, and that this is so is basically due to that low self-esteem neglected and long forgotten.

"A person cannot be comfortable without their own approval."

**-Mark Twain-**

**Low self-esteem and self-sabotage, when we have been undervaluing for years**

We know that low self-esteem and self-sabotage are related. However, what is the first? Is the low appreciation towards our person, or is it that negative internal dialogue that weakens self-esteem more and more? We cannot separate one thing from the other, because everything is a continuum, everything responds to a mental approach focused on failure, insecurity, and lack of self-confidence.

In this way, some can say with all the good intentions of the world to that friend, to that coworker that of 'you have to love yourself more, you have to take care of your self-esteem.' However, they may not know how to perceive themselves in any other way. That low self-esteem may be present almost from childhood, shaping a type of approach and mental pattern that is very difficult to tear down — there where a negative attribution and self-sabotage is almost chronic.

Thus, in a study conducted by Jennifer Campbell, from the University of Vancouver, Canada, he points out something relevant. Self-esteem clarifies self-concept. Promoting healthy self-esteem will help us build a resilient personality with better resources.

On the contrary, if fears, insecurity, or fear of not being up to the expectations of others weigh too heavily since our early years, it will not be easy to change our approaches from one day to the next. It requires, without a doubt, deeper craftsmanship.

**There is a 'Trojan' in your thinking, get rid of it**

When low self-esteem and self-sabotage are those eternal constants in our lives, we must become aware of something. There are certain 'Trojan' or viruses in our mental focus. They are specific codes of thought that are installed in our mind with a very clear purpose: to interfere with projects, destroy dreams, become someone we do not like.

Don't blame your education or what other people have told you or made you believe about yourself. Self-esteem is erected by you and only you, depending on how you speak to yourself and how you interpret each experience, each event that surrounds you.

Eliminate those Trojans by sanitizing your internal dialogue. Eliminate the 'I can not,' the 'I am going to go wrong, I am not worth it, they will think of me that, surely I fail.' Don't invalidate yourself as a human being; if you are here, it is for some reason, so clarify your goals, your purposes, your reason for being.

**Doing nothing is also self-sabotage, move**

When we talk about self-sabotage, we instantly visualize someone thinking about negative things about himself. Now, we must bear in mind that self-sabotage is a prism with many faces. One of them, perhaps one of the most relevant, is procrastination, not reacting to what hurts, worries, or scares me. Leaving projects, leaving something for fear of failing or not daring, etc., all this also ends up undermining our self-esteem.

If we really want a change and also enhance our positive self-perception, let us intelligently dispose of our forces. Being proactive, finishing what we started, acquiring commitments, and finding ways to enjoy trails, generates high satisfaction.

**Against low self-esteem and self-sabotage, responsibility**

To overcome low self-esteem and self-sabotage, you need large doses of responsibility with oneself. No one else will do it for us. Moreover, in our day to day, things will always happen that will put us to the test, which will require us to know how to react, adapt, and respond. Doing it in the best way is our obligation.

Therefore, to achieve strong self-esteem, it is not enough to love each other very much, a vital history is also necessary for which the edges are integrated - errors, traumas, disappointments, etc. - and assumed the dissonances and contradictions. At the same time, it is a priority as well, that we learn to be compassionate with ourselves to tolerate mistakes but demanding enough to overcome each day.

Self-sabotage is the echo of a voice that does not love us, and as such, we must free ourselves from it as soon as possible. Life is already complicated enough for us to live inside us with someone who likes to invalidate us. Such work requires time and perseverance, a firm commitment to practice daily without rest and without surrender. Let's always keep it in mind.

# CHAPTER 8

# PSYCHOLOGY 101

# Psychology

Psychology or psychology is a social science and academic discipline focused on the analysis and understanding of human behavior and mental processes experienced by individuals and by social groups during specific times and situations.

Psychology has a vast field of study, since it focuses on the human mind and experience, from various perspectives, currents and methodologies. Some of them are closer to the hard sciences and the use of the scientific method, while others do not consider it appropriate for the object of study, and prefer to build their own methods and approaches.

In this sense, this social science is interested in the processes of perception, motivation, attention, intelligence, learning, thinking, personality, love, awareness and unconsciousness, but also interpersonal relationships and by the biochemical functioning of the brain.

The professional practice of psychology, on the other hand, is usually divided between academic research, education, and educational innovation, or clinical exercise, that is, therapeutic work to understand and solve various emotional, psychological, or affective diseases in their patients. The latter is known as psychotherapy.

Psychology should not be confused with psychiatry. The latter is a branch of medicine that studies the biochemical behavior of the brain, without generally dealing with the emotional or experiential content of patients. Nor should it be done with psychoanalysis, which is an interpretive and therapeutic discipline derived from the studies of the human mind of Sigmund Freud.

# Origin of psychology

Psychology is a relatively new science, detached from philosophy since the eighteenth century, following the philosophical doctrines of empiricism, which began to understand human behavior as a series of stimuli and responses determined by our biology.

Thus was born psychophysiology, the precursor of the psychological field. With the entry of formal sciences into the panorama of knowledge, the possibility of psychology no longer merely theoretical, but even experimental begins.

The first experimental psychology laboratory was founded at the University of Leipzig, Germany, in 1879. From then on, various branches of theoretical and practical exploration of the human mind would emerge, inaugurating a very vast and diverse area of knowledge as it is today.

# Branches of psychology

Psychology has a huge number of branches and divisions, which can be grouped into two sets according to their common characteristics, in this way:

**Basic psychology.** Located as a field of knowledge between the biological of man and the social or human, it focuses on understanding and gathering information about the basic processes of human thought. It comprises the following sub-branches:

- Cognitive psychology. Study the mental processes that allow the knowledge, that is, experience. The perception, the memory, the language, and thought are their areas of interest.
- Psychology of learning. It is dedicated to the study of the processes of adaptation and more or less permanent change in the individual, that is, how human beings learn.
- Evolutionary Psychology. He studies the different stages of growth and development of the human psyche throughout his life.
- Psychopathology. The study of "abnormalities" or disorders of the psyche, from an eminently descriptive method.
- Psychology of art. Study the phenomena of creativity, creation, and artistic expression from the human mind.
- Personality psychology. Try to build models of understanding the human personality.

**Applied Psychology.** Also called professional psychology, it is the basic psychological knowledge put at the service of solving specific problems of society. It comprises the following sub-branches:

- Clinical Psychology. It is the one that deals with patients, attending to their mental and emotional sufferings and allowing them to lead a life as functional as possible according to the case.
- Educational psychology. It is focused on the learning and growth of the individual that collaborates with the construction of school habits and environments that are more conducive to form the coming generations.
- Child psychology. Together with the child-youth, they specialize in emotional or mental problems during the early stages of human life.
- Social psychology. It focuses on human groups and human interactions, emphasizing the importance of the environment in the configuration of the psyche.
- Industrial psychology. Similar to the social one, but applied to the diverse work environments and mental situations involved in the work.
- Forensic psychology. Collaborate with justice in the mental understanding of criminals, homicides, and other borderline situations.
- Sports psychology. He applies his knowledge to the athletic and sports field to understand what happens there mentally and emotionally.

# Humanistic Psychology, What Does It Consist Of?

Humanistic psychology has as its main characteristic to consider the human being as a whole, knowing that multiple factors intervene in mental health, personal growth, and self-realization. Among them converge and interrelate aspects such as emotions, body, feelings, behavior, thoughts, etc.

We are not mistaken if we say that this approach, this theoretical and practical perspective stands today as one of the most remarkable psychological currents. It is a legacy that is worth knowing, and that can undoubtedly provide us with valuable tools: self-knowledge and self-discovery, skills for change, social relationships, strengthening self-esteem...

« I realize that if I were stable, prudent, and static, I would live in death. Therefore, I accept confusion, uncertainty, fear, and emotional ups and downs because that is the price I am willing to pay for a fluid, perplexed, and exciting life.

**-Carl Rogers -**

Few approaches to psychology directly focus on the positive features and behaviors of the human being. It is from these dimensions that we must start to promote healing, growth, and change. Within ourselves, there is a highly valuable capacity that can guarantee our well-being and balance.

## How does humanist psychology arise?

Kirk J. Schneider psychologist, psychotherapist and one of the most renowned exponents of humanist psychology explain in a study published in the American Psychologist that today this approach, together with that of positive psychology, configure an advance within the field of behavioral sciences and psychotherapy itself.

We are facing an effective current to treat a lot of psychological disorders. It is also useful as a growth tool and to improve family relationships. Thus, and in spite of how consolidated it is possible to say that this current of psychology is relatively young.

Humanistic psychology appears in the mid-twentieth century as an alternative to the two main forces: behaviorism and psychoanalysis. Its purpose was to give a different response, addressing the problems of the human being and offering a perspective from the field of health, rather than disease.

## The freedom of the individual and existentialism

This perspective opted for a more holistic vision and less focused on the pathological, on the influences of the past or the environment to enhance the positive side of human nature. Thus, theories such as Abraham Maslow's about needs and motivations established a basis for shaping another kind of philosophy. She was joined by names as relevant as that of Carl Rogers, who emphasized, for example, the freedom of individuals when taking the course of their lives.

In this way, the humanist therapists of this era firmly believed that people are intrinsically motivated to self-realize, to move towards their own goals, and thus achieve the healing, wisdom, or personal summit to which each one aspires.

The person is also considered as an individual being, who needs to be attended in a multidimensional and personalized way. The roots of humanistic psychology are in turn within the philosophical current of European existentialism, an approach led by names as relevant as:

- **Jean-Paul Sartre:** «Man is born free, responsible, and without excuses.»
- **Jean Jacques Rousseau:** «Man is good by nature; it is a society that corrupts him.»
- **Erich Fromm:** «If I am what I have and what I have I lose, then who am I?»
- **Viktor Frankl**: «Man is self-realized to the same extent that he commits himself to the fulfillment of the meaning of his life.»

These authors have a vision of the human condition based on freedom, the meaning of life, emotions, and responsibility. They consider the individual as being responsible for their life and their actions, capable of finding their path to freedom.

## Main precursors of humanistic psychology

We talked about them just now: Abraham Maslow and Carl Rogers can be considered as the main precursors of humanistic psychology. Let's get to know more about them.

### · Abraham Maslow

Most of us know Abraham Maslow for his famous pyramid of human needs. It establishes a hierarchy with different levels of needs and motivations, starting from the most basic (physiological), until reaching the top where the self-realization would be: concept created by Maslow when considering that when the human being has satisfied all his needs It is when he reaches a stage of development of his vital impulse.

"The basic element of the field of knowledge is an intimate and direct experience. (...) There is no substitute for experience. "

**- Abraham Maslow -**

Maslow's contribution to psychology is immense, especially as regards the field of personal growth. Today, we continue to review and update concepts such as self-realization. And an example of this is the study conducted by Professor Willard Mittelman of the University of Georgia, where he proposes replacing this term with "experiential openness."

### · Carl Rogers

Carl Rogers opted for a novel vision of doing therapy, that which facilitates a more direct relationship with the "client" (a term coined within psychology because it is considered more appropriate than "patient"). In his book, Client-centered therapy shows how, in his clinical experience, he rejects directive techniques, showing a closer relationship with his clients, thus favoring a more meaningful encounter with themselves.

His contribution to psychology from this perspective is of great value since he considers the individual capable of finding within him all the resources necessary to maintain a balance in his life.

For Rogers, people who go through a moment are because they are "asleep," and they need to wake up through their inner wisdom. The therapist serves as a guide for them to find their answers since they rely on the self-healing ability of each individual.

**Characteristics of humanistic psychology**

**Contemplate a broad and holistic perspective**

It is characterized by seeing the person as a whole, globally. Each of the aspects having the same relevance: thoughts, body, emotions, and the spiritual realm. These aspects interrelate and converge with each other. They are the main way for the individual to find himself.

**Human existence occurs in an interpersonal context**

Therefore, they consider that the relationship with others is very important and necessary, taking into account the context in which it is produced for the individual development of the human being.

## The capacity for decision and personal development

People can make their own decisions, to take responsibility for themselves and to undertake development and deployment of their potential.

Also, personal development is promoted and facilitated. The psychologist serves as a tool for the person, so that she, through her abilities, can come to understand and develop.

## The value of inner wisdom

People have an innate tendency to self-realization. The human being can rely on the wisdom that starts from within since all healing is found in his answers. For this, it is necessary to understand that it is not necessary to control the environment or control one's emotions until repressed.

To conclude, humanistic psychology focuses on the individual from a global vision, understanding that all aspects that make up the human being are important. He is considered a unique being, responsible for his own experience, capable of becoming aware of his resources to develop, reach self-realization, and discover his potentialities.

# What has applied psychology?

Psychology is often conceived as a large tree with infinite branches were to try to understand human behavior. Thus, and among all this set of derivations and sheets, a particularly useful one is distinguished: we speak of applied psychology, one that tries to give concrete solutions to the problems that occur in our daily lives.

It is possible that more than one reader feels somewhat surprised. Isn't that what psychology has always done? Is not this science has focused since its inception in help and support to respond to the needs of common and complex human beings? Well, it should be said that as surprising as we think the answer is no, it was not always the case.

«Intelligence consists not only in knowledge but also in the skill of applying knowledge in practice.»

**-Aristotle-**

Psychology in its origins was more focused on the collection of information and the compression of psychological processes as elementary as attention, memory, learning, or language... All this exciting, immense, and always constantly expanding area configures what is known as "basic psychology."

For its part, it was not until the late nineteenth and early twentieth centuries when, thanks to the German-American psychologist Hugo Münsterberg, there was a new leap in the history of psychology. This vast science was finally oriented towards the search for practical and real solutions for the human being, using all that knowledge generated by basic psychology to transform our scenarios, to enhance the learning, well-being, and health of people. As we can see, it is almost impossible to conceive both areas separately. Basic psychology and applied psychology are two fundamental branches of the same tree. A spectacular tree that will never stop growing to improve our environments and our quality of life.

## Hugo Münsterberg: an objective man who laid the foundations of applied psychology

They tell the biographers of Hugo Münsterberg that he used to read Kant and that although at first, he had a good relationship with William James after he proposed to work in his Harvard University psychology laboratory, things between them did not end too much well. It is said that William James had some interest in investigating the so-called paranormal phenomena, something that the disciple of Wilhelm Wundt could not conceive and accept as being a staunch lover of the objective, and in essence, of the practical.

Münsterberg cataloged everything that escaped the logical and the tangible as the "psychology of abracadabra." Perhaps because of this, and knowing that his main interest was to increase productivity in companies, he always felt a certain tension with those academic colleagues who understood psychology from the laboratory. From the point of view of observation and experimentation in order to publish an article and perhaps collapse some theory preconceived by other colleagues.

If there was a reason why Hugo Münsterberg laid the foundations of applied psychology, it was for a very specific objective: he wanted to improve the skills of workers in that context where industry and Taylorism already demanded new profiles. People fitter and qualified to A more complex work environment.

Thus, and although Münsterberg passed away early with just over 50 years, his contribution to the field of applied psychology was decisive, while immense. He established the origin of industrial psychology, developed multiple tests on professional capacity, and even laid the foundations of legal psychology by creating a scale to assess the reliability of testimonies.

**The different aspects of applied psychology**

We said at the beginning that much of the tools and knowledge used by applied psychology start directly from basic psychology. Now, it should be said that as always happens when we carry out any practical work, the application and development of work end up generating new knowledge, new data, and concepts. Therefore, it is not difficult to understand that many times applied psychology can gain some independence from that sister branch that is basic psychology, and that tries to give rise to it.

In this way, we also understand that applied psychology can have infinite fields of action, areas that cover many of our most everyday contexts; and where, thanks to its immersion, we can find solutions, enhance skills, improve processes, innovate, etc. Let's see some examples below.

That theory that finds no practical application in life is acrobatics of thought.

**-Swami Vivekananda-**

- Health Psychology. Although this area has points in common with clinical psychology, it can be said that they are two different disciplines. Health psychology analyzes the relationship between behavior and physical disorders and seeks to prevent and treat different diseases.
- Clinical Psychology. It focuses its field of work on preventing and treating dysfunctional behavior to improve our quality of life and our mental well-being.
- Sports psychology. It seeks to enhance the performance of athletes, reducing, for example, anxiety and improving teamwork of sports teams.
- The psychology of organizations. This is, together with clinical psychology, the two best-known aspects of applied psychology. In this case, what is sought is to improve the work environment, solve problems, train, train, enhance skills, manage the human resources of any organization...
- Educational psychology. We are facing another important area, where applied psychology uses

basic to improve teaching, methodologies to understand how students learn and provide them with better resources and mechanisms in their day to day.

- Environmental Psychology. In this case, we have an area as essential as it is interesting to understand how people relate to their environment and how the environment itself can affect our behavior.
- Forensic psychology. In this case, the professional's work is not limited only to the investigation of crimes or any criminal act. The validity of testimonies, custody conflicts, attention to victims, etc. is also analyzed.
- Advertising psychology. Something we all know is that advertising is an integral part of the consumer economy. Understanding what drives the buyer to choose certain products, knowing which unconscious processes regulate their desires and needs, are critical aspects of this exciting area of psychology.

As we see, each field of action gives rise to a differentiated profile in the exercise of the profession. They are aspects of applied psychology that are part of our society where we certainly lack many more fields to be detailed, such as emergency psychology, road safety, aging, etc. They are only small examples that give us to understand the multiple scenarios where psychology can be valuable, where good professionals will always try to respond to any need, to any problem.

# Wisdom from psychology

Wisdom, which is usually understood as an exclusive product of experience, goes further. Thus, this section presents definitions given by different authors, such as Sternberg, while certain ideas are demystified, and the problem of their measurement develops.

Wisdom, beyond popular conception, has been studied by intelligence experts and psychologists. Wisdom can be defined in scientific terms, beyond the attribution of knowledge that we usually give to our elders.

In this section, we are going to talk about what the science of psychology understands by wisdom. It is a difficult concept to study because of the diffusion of its limits and how complicated it is to use scientific methodology with internal elements.

**What is wisdom, according to psychology?**

Wisdom can be defined as a set of knowledge that is possessed in the pragmatics of life at expert levels. Many have been the authors who have tried to identify the components associated with wisdom.

The components that are usually grouped around wisdom are:

- Interpersonal skills: Level of knowledge, sensitivity, and sociability when interacting with other people.

Interpersonal skills lead one to adapt to the needs of the interlocutor and squeeze the interaction with the other in the most effective way.

- Judgment and communication skills: Wisdom, which is usually related to experience, implies knowledge and advice. Therefore, wise people are individuals capable of advising on problems and giving pragmatic solutions that others would not reach.

- Understanding: Wise people, having been able to cultivate emotion and along with their vital experiences, are individuals who understand and can empathize.

- General competence: This would be the most known or attributed to the wisdom component. Wise people are intelligent, educated, have high knowledge in different fields, and know how to communicate it.

**Does wisdom necessarily imply knowledge?**

Experts allude that the two most relevant factors of wisdom are exceptional understanding and the skills of judgment and communication. Therefore, there may be wise people but, because of vital vicissitudes, do not possess great knowledge about the world.

All the aforementioned components, therefore, appeal to a construct of wisdom that alludes to affective and interpersonal aspects. In other words, a definition that goes beyond the cognitive.

### · Wisdom according to Holliday and Chandler (1986)

For these two authors, wisdom implies sagacity, involvement with others, consideration, insight, intuition, knowing one's limitations, reason and logic, experience, logical mind, good problem solving and error learning. The wise person is an information seeker who uses the data he has well.

The definition of Holliday and Chandler tends more to relate wisdom to cognitive factors and aptitudes that allow a person the proper and brilliant problem-solving.

### · Wisdom according to Sternberg (1985)

Sternberg, on the other hand, defines the wise as someone sensitive, sociable, with good judgment and communication skills, who understands life, who has learned from experience and is able to combine different points of view.

In addition to all these interpersonal and emotional faculties, it also defines the wise person as someone intelligent, cultivated, and with great general skills.

### How do you analyze wisdom from science?

In some way, we can assess the level of a person in the dimension through standardized tests and qualitative procedures. There would be two large groups:

- **Planning tasks:** Subjects are presented with a test in which a person has to make a decision. This decision is about life in certain circumstances. It can be a younger person, with aspects to take into account in the decision making... In this test, the person responds aloud with a plan that covers what he could do, what would be the impact of said decision in the coming years, and what other information you need to make the decision that may not be found in the presentation of the task.

- **Review tasks:** Situations arise in which different people - who adopted different paths at a crossroads - have to review the decisions made. The subjects evaluated reexamine those decisions, responding aloud. They reconstruct and evaluate what the protagonists of the story would say as they grew older.

- **Task example:** Tadeo wants to get married

An example of a task to evaluate wisdom could be the following:

"Tadeo is an 18-year-old boy who decides to marry her boyfriend, whom she has known for nine months."

Based on this statement, the person has to think out loud what Tadeo should consider making this decision. Reconstructs, from Tadeo, the history, the moments of it, possible explanations that have led him to make that decision and evaluations about it.

## Can you train wisdom?

Many are the authors who have spoken of the components of wisdom, although there are fewer who agree. However, this does not take away so that it is being analyzed how a person can improve in those components on which there is a greater consensus.

For example, what it is about promoting in decision making is contextualism, relativism, and uncertainty. The only decision-making factor that has been trained is relativism, and the calm or restraint it offers. However, the goal of "training" wisdom still seems too risky.

## What does science forget?

One part that does not usually measure standardized tests is emotional and affective factors. You are better suited to evaluate different dimensions of intelligence, such as logical-mathematical intelligence or spatial intelligence.

On the other hand, to date, several definitions of wisdom survive without there being a very broad consensus around one of them. It is an open field, and therefore, it is a complicated task to measure it. This disparity in assessing wisdom can mean that we currently have very biased results referring to the different groups that have been studied.

# Can knowledge be inherited?

An extraordinary study conducted at the University of Tel Aviv on the heritability of knowledge has just been published. The results of the investigation call into question the famous Weismann barrier, one of the basic principles of biology...

A recent investigation carried out at the University of Tel Aviv has just put in check one of the basic principles of biology: the Weismann barrier. This study is the first step to future research on the heritability of knowledge; that is, the study opens the door to the possibility of inheriting the knowledge of past generations.

The team of Professor Oded Rechavi, from the Department of Neurobiology of the Faculty of Life Sciences Wise, together with the Sagol School of Neuroscience, has discovered an RNA-based mechanism that encourages the response of neurons to the environment to be inheritable. An acquired information that would affect the behavior of the progeny.

The experiment, which was presented on June 6, 2019, was carried out on a species of worms, the nematodes (Caenorhabditis elegans). The team showed how nervous system cells could transmit information to subsequent generations of worms.

## The germline and the controversy of inheriting the knowledge

It seems that the mechanism of RNA regulation would allow the nervous system of living beings to communicate with the germline. This line would affect the behavior of the following generations. This is the great novelty that this study brings.

So, if this research is right, it would mean that the nervous system can control the progeny. The discovery collides head-on with Weismann's barrier, one of the most accepted principles of biology, although very controversial and widely discussed in recent decades.

### The Weismann Barrier

Weismann's barrier is the theory that ensures that the acquired characteristics are features of soma cells and that in no case are they transmitted to future generations. This barrier is what differentiates, according to Weismann, the body's soma cells and germ cells (ovules and sperm cells).

Freiburg A. Weismann was a German biologist and geneticist, who presented his conclusions on hereditary information, the inheritance germplasm, in the book published in 1892.

According to their theories, they affirm that the changes in the germinal plasma produced by environmental influences would only affect the inheritance if they occur in the germinal plasma. Still, they would not do so if they occur in the soma (body) of the cell.

Many have since been the voices in the academic world that have argued that the somato-germinal barrier does not work that way. However, this theory has been taken for years as the basis for rejecting the inheritance of acquired characters.

**The investigation**

The recently presented study has turned the Weismann barrier. The most advanced systems have been used for this study. The latest CRISPR-Cas9 gene-editing tool was used to create a variant form of a mutant gene or allele. A genetically encoded calcium indicator (GECI) and calcium image analysis, GCaMp2, have also been used.

For this purpose, worms were designed to produce RDE-4-dependent endo-siRNA only in neurons. The purpose was to understand the inheritable effects of neuronal RNApn (small nuclear RNA). Genetically encoded calcium analyzes allowed the observation of neuronal activity through optogenetic systems.

**Inherit knowledge: how it works**

The research concluded that the RNA of the neurons regulates the germline genes and controls the behavior of future generations. This mechanism would control the expression of the germline gene for several generations.

More specifically, it is the neuronal RDE-4 that controls chemotaxis for at least three generations. It would do so through the ArgonauteHRDE-1 that is restricted to the germline.

## An open the door to research

This discovery about the mechanism of RNA that makes communication between the cells of the nervous system and germ cells possible to allow the heritability of the information acquired in the following generations can change the way we understand the process.

New research in the future could confirm the functioning of this mechanism in the rest of the animals and in the human being. Undoubtedly, the implications of this study on the knowledge we have about genetics, evolution, epigenetics, and the heritability of intelligence are enormous.

# Similarities And Differences Between Psychology And Sociology

Social psychology and sociology, could you say what differentiates them? Although they may seem the same, they are different. On the other hand, it is no less true that they share some elements in their definition and that the birth of one depended, in part, on the other. At first, there were only sociology and psychology. A part of psychology was interested in social and group processes, thus emerging social psychology. Therefore, the names are related. Social psychology comes from the integration of psychology and sociology.

Sociology, on the other hand, was also interested in the individual processes that psychology studied. The interaction between subjects and their environment became the object of reflection by sociologists, thus moving away from other macro-sociological approaches. Therefore, we can find that there has been a great influence of one over the other - and vice versa - in the evolution of both so that its evolution is largely common.

At present, both fields of knowledge in their evolution have tended towards specialization. Each has invested its efforts in increasingly specific and particular aspects. The result has been that both have ended up isolating themselves. Thus, sociologists have focused on macro variables, such as social structure (Bourdieu, 1998) or migrations (Castles, 2003), while social psychology has focused on micro variables such as group identity (Tajfel and Turner, 2005) or influence (Cialdini, 2001).

## A love-hate relationship

It is noteworthy that both sciences share a common object of study, human behavior. However, social psychology would become a branch of psychology that studies how the environment directly or indirectly influences the behavior and behavior of the human being (Allport, 1985). For its part, sociology is a social science that is dedicated to the systematic study of society, social action, and the groups that comprise it (Furfey, 1953). You could say that both study relationships between people, but from different perspectives.

The fact that each one has its watchtower in different places means that one can get rich from the other, while the differences between the two are accentuated. One of the main differences between the two is that psychology studies the effect of the social on the individual, while sociology focuses on the collective phenomena themselves. In other words, social psychology studies human behavior at the level of the individual and sociology at the group level.

## · Social psychology

Social psychology has as its ultimate goal the analysis of the interaction between the individual and society (Moskovici and Markova, 2006). These interaction processes take place at different levels, which are usually divided into intrapersonal, interpersonal, intragroup, and intergroup processes.

In short, processes between people and between groups. In the field of interpersonal processes, the differences between people, information processing. How this information is used within the groups is studied. As for intergroup processes, between groups, the emphasis is placed on the study of the role of groups in the construction of people's identity.

Social psychology takes social phenomena into account but does not focus their study on them. Instead, analyze how these social phenomena have an effect on the individual. Social psychology tries to understand how most individuals are affected by social factors, regardless of their individual personality differences.

## · The sociology

Sociology, in its research, studies how organizations and institutions that make up the social structure are created, maintained, or changed (Tezanos, 2006). In turn, it also studies the effect that different social structures have on the behavior of groups and individuals; and the changes that occur in these structures as a cause of social interactions (Lucas Marín, 2006).

In other words of Richard Osborne (2005), " sociology is to

explain something that seems obvious (how our society works) to people who believe it is simple and who do not understand how complicated it really is ." The acts we perform on a day-to-day basis sometimes have explanations that we would never think about.

**Great representatives of both fields**

Although, both in social psychology and in sociology, the representatives of these fields are counted by millions, some have excelled. Unable to honor all the great researchers who have left their mark, here are some of the theories and methods left by two of the best-known representatives of both fields and that will help to understand the differences between the two sciences:

- Pierre Bourdieu (1998) is known, among other things, for introducing the concept of habitus. He will tell us that the habitus is a set of schemes through which we perceive the world and act in it. The habitus has a great influence on our thoughts, perceptions, and actions. The habitus becomes the fundamental dimension that explains the social class. The social class is integrated from the characteristic habits of it. The performance of actions is what places us in a certain social class.
- Henri Tajfel, together with John Turner (2005), developed the theory of social identity. According to this theory, through categorization processes, we end up identifying with groups whose norms are going to modulate our behaviors. The greater the

identification with a group, the more willing we will be to follow the rules of that group and even make sacrifices so that they continue to be maintained.

While Bourdieu proposes that the schemes from which we perceive the world are going to determine our behaviors, Tajfel interprets that group membership is going to be what determines their behavior according to the group's norms. As mentioned, they study the same thing but from different perspectives.

# Why is psychology important?

Due to the breadth of the field of psychology, its importance depends largely on the specific application to which we refer. However, in this section, we will reflect on the relevance of psychology at a general level, emphasizing some of its key contributions.

## 1. To understand living beings

Psychological theories are fundamental to explain the behavior of animals, especially people: any activity produced in human society is likely to be analyzed from psychology since it will always involve the participation of basic mental processes. Concerning the study of human groups, social psychology is particularly important.

Behavior analysis is not only interesting in itself for a large number of people, but also allows the knowledge acquired to be applied to many different fields. Especially within the social and natural sciences such as medicine, sociology, economics, history, political science, demography, linguistics, veterinary medicine, or zoology.

## 2. To increase the quality of life

Many people believe that the ultimate goal of psychology is to increase the well-being and quality of life of others. Although other professionals have different conceptions, the truth is that service to other people has been a central aspect of the development of psychology and continues to be so today.

Psychology is useful for enhancing mental health and personal growth, but the benefits of this science are not limited to the psyche. Health psychology, for example, seeks physical well-being and disease prevention through the acquisition of healthy behavioral habits, a key aspect that medicine tends to set aside.

## 3. To improve relationships

The knowledge derived from psychological science is very important for the improvement of human relationships. Thus, it is the psychologists who are most qualified to improve the social skills of shy people, to mediate in cases of divorce, or to intervene in mobbing and bullying, among other functions.

## 4. To enhance professional performance

In today's societies, performance and productivity are extremely valuable on a professional level, and more and more people realize that having psychologists in their work team clearly enhances the results. Human resources, organizational psychology, and sports psychology are good examples of this role.